"In reading this book, I'm struck by the way Crystal speaks the truth with vast amounts of both humility and love. Her voice reminds you that you're not alone in your fears or your failures. *Love-Centered Parenting* will not only help you give yourself grace, but help you cling to the grace of Christ in a way that will make you a better—and freer—parent."

—Sissy Goff, LPC-MHSP, director of child and adolescent counseling, Daystar Counseling Ministries; author of *Raising Worry-Free Girls*

"*Love-Centered Parenting* is a book that belongs on every parent's bedside table. What makes this book so powerful and unique is that Crystal writes honestly and humbly from her own experience of growing from a mama who thought she had to get it all right to a mama who's learned to trust the transforming power of God's grace in her kids' lives. *Love-Centered Parenting* will inspire you to rest in your freedom in Christ and empower you to reflect God's heart to your kids."

—Jeannie Cunnion, author of *Mom Set Free*

"Full of real-life examples and practical steps to take toward change, *Love-Centered Parenting* is the go-to guide for every mom who feels lost in motherhood. With heartfelt humility and vulnerability, Crystal gives us permission to not have it all together and ultimately points us to the One who does. I really love this book!"

—Ruth Schwenk, founder of TheBetterMom.com and author of *The Better Mom Devotional* and *Pressing Pause*

"If you're at the end of your rope . . . if you've done everything right and it's still all wrong . . . if you're ready for a full pivot from what has been to what can be . . . this is your book. Crystal's honest, brave story of redemption, and the God who brings beauty from ashes, will reshape and challenge the way you think about parenting. This is a must-read for real parents who need real help."

—Brooke McGlothlin, cofounder of Million Praying Moms, author of *Gospel-Centered Mom: The Freeing Truth about What Your Kids Really Need*

"*Love-Centered Parenting* is about parenting with humility—and since humility brings wisdom, it's what every parent needs! By bravely sharing her story and what God revealed during a dark season, Crystal gives hope to moms who desire stronger relationships and healthier dynamics at home. Crystal's advice is practical, timeless, and Christ centered. This beautiful love story about a mother's personal journey will inspire you to generously give grace and love your children well!"

—Kari Kampakis, author of *Love Her Well: 10 Ways to Find Joy and Connection with Your Teenage Daughter*

"What if we parented knowing we are loved and set free? Crystal not only asks readers that question but relays how it's possible as she vulnerably shares relatable stories from her own parenting journey. You'll find yourself implementing the shared strategies before you even turn the last page."

—Erin Port, creator of Simple Purposeful Living

"The message Crystal shares in this book was exactly what I needed to hear right now as a mom of four little ones. It touched me deeply, brought me to tears at times, and ultimately left me feeling encouraged and equipped with godly, practical wisdom for my parenting journey. I highly recommend this book and will be rereading it for sure."

—Rebekah Gaspar, creator of TheTexMexMom.com, stay-at-home mother of four

"As a mom of eight kids, I have read countless formula-centered parenting books only to be disappointed in the results. Through heartfelt, personal experiences, Crystal takes us right back to Scripture to remind us who we are in Christ first, so we are free to pursue the heart of love-centered parenting."

—Julie Schultz, homeschool mom

"*Love-Centered Parenting* is encouraging and powerful and has caused me to reevaluate how I am raising my children. Crystal explains the changes she made in an eloquent and easy-to-understand manner. She has given me hope that I can make similar changes and grow closer to my children."

—Lindsay Jones, real estate broker, Sell with Jones Real Estate Professionals; mother of two

"In *Love-Centered Parenting*, through the lens of growing in our own relationship with Christ, Crystal pulls from her parenting experiences and shares a wealth of practical wisdom that will challenge your perspective on what it looks like to lavishly love your children! A needed and impactful message for any parent!"

—Bethany Beasley

"Crystal's journey of parenting through love and grace will bring you to tears. Both of sorrow and joy. Parenting is hard, but with the many tools she has laid out so beautifully this book will leave you ready to take it on with passion!"

—Nichole Jordan, mother of seven and foster mom to thirteen

"Raw, vulnerable, and beautifully crafted, *Love-Centered Parenting* instills a feeling of hope for parents who are tired or feel like they don't measure up. Crystal walks hand in hand with us and teaches how to parent from a place of love as we learn to parent alongside Jesus Christ."

—Micah Klug, homeschooling mom of five

"While reading this book, I never felt judged. Instead, I felt loved. I felt seen, heard, and empowered. Crystal opens her heart up in a vulnerable and heart-wrenching way that only another mama can. This book is truly the best gift you could give to a parent in your life."

—Kathryn Owens, realtor, Brooke Group Real Estate with eXp Realty; music teacher turned stay-at-home mother of two, now turned realtor

"*Refreshing* is the best way to describe *Love-Centered Parenting*. Crystal blesses others by encouraging them through her honesty and heartfelt lessons as a mom. Parenting for my kids and not my reputation, along with her sharing how to *lean in and love* our kids has blessed me beyond measure."

—Stephanie Lloyd, *Choose Happy Podcast—Life, Love and Family*, wife, homeschool mom and podcaster, mother of five and stepmother of three

"As a severe–food-allergy mom, this book has been a life changer. Crystal shared truth and encouragement through relatable and raw personal stories. I found myself saying, 'Same here!' again and again, which inspired me to put her thoughts into action in my parenting and life. It's a must-read!"

—Corinna Meckelborg, founder of Friendly Pantry Consulting, mother of two

"I wish I had read this book when my kids were younger, but there are plenty of practical tips reassuring me that I can still make real improvements in my relationships with my kids. I appreciate Crystal's faith-based, practical encouragement and storytelling throughout."

—Dawn Aldridge, owner of ChoosingReal.com

"Crystal masterfully uses her vulnerable story to help us parent from a place of love-centered rest, rather than performance-based stress. Filled with practical tools and heartfelt encouragement, this is the book I wish I had read when my four adult children were babies."

—Kimberlee Stokes, owner of ThePeacefulMom.com

"Do you remember bringing home your first baby from the hospital and thinking, 'Now what?' There is no one-size-fits-all strategy for raising good kids. But in this guide, Crystal offers sound advice and practical strategies for loving and guiding your children well through relationship rather than rules."

—Becca Thomas, RN, BeccaThomas.com, mother of three

"Crystal has done a beautiful job diving into what our job as parents should be, not what we think it should be. Her breakdown of ways we can be love centered in our parenting and sharing what that looks like for her and her family is an invaluable gift!"

—Lora Vann, work-from-home mom of two

# LOVE-
## CENTERED
## PARENTING

# LOVE-
## CENTERED
## PARENTING

The No-Fail Guide
to Launching Your Kids

## CRYSTAL PAINE

BETHANYHOUSE
*a division of Baker Publishing Group*
Minneapolis, Minnesota

Published by Bethany House Publishers
11400 Hampshire Avenue South
Bloomington, Minnesota 55438
www.bethanyhouse.com

Bethany House Publishers is a division of
Baker Publishing Group, Grand Rapids, Michigan

Printed in the United States of America

Library of Congress Cataloging-in-Publication Data
Names: Paine, Crystal, author.
Title: Love-centered parenting : the no-fail guide to launching your kids / Crystal Paine.
Description: Minneapolis, Minnesota : Bethany House Publishers, a division of Baker Publishing Group, [2021] | Includes bibliographical references.
Identifiers: LCCN 2020046864 | ISBN 9780764237225 (cloth) | ISBN 9780764237232 (paper) | ISBN 9781493429981 (ebook)
Subjects: LCSH: Parenting—Religious aspects—Christianity. | Child rearing—Religious aspects—Christianity.
Classification: LCC BV4529 .P345 2021 | DDC 248.8/45—dc23
LC record available at https://lccn.loc.gov/2020046864

Cover design by Kara Klontz

All emojis designed by OpenMoji—the open-source emoji and icon project. License: CC BY-SA 4.0

21  22  23  24  25  26  27        7  6  5  4  3  2  1

# Contents

9

# Contents

# Introduction

I never, ever expected I would write a book on parenting. But the reality is that I never could have imagined how much my life and perspective would change in the last four years.

Four years ago, I was kind of coasting along as a mom. We had made it past the diapers and sippy cup stage. Everyone was potty trained (praise Jesus!). Everyone could buckle and unbuckle themselves when we got in and out of the car (hallelujah!). And everyone could make their own breakfast and lunches. (Can I get an amen?)

I finally felt like life was running fairly smoothly and I had re-learned how to sleep through the night again. (After seven years of either being pregnant or nursing—or both—I had forgotten what getting six hours of sleep all in one fell swoop even felt like!)

My kids seemed happy. Life felt pretty calm and organized. I was finding my groove. Or so I thought.

And then, in one day's time, the facade came crashing down and I had to face the reality that I had been royally missing the mark in my mothering.

I had to go back to square one as a mom. I was confronted with the harsh reality that the way I was parenting was not about my kids' hearts but about my own reputation. As a result, I was wounding my children and setting them up for failure.

The events of that day blindsided me—as I'll tell you about in chapter 1. But they also showed me that I had to relearn how to parent.

This journey has been excruciatingly painful and also deeply healing.

It has brought me to my knees before the Lord as never before.

It has stripped me of all vestiges of pride.

It has changed me to my core.

It has transformed the way I walk with, love on, and parent my kids.

And it has given me a depth of joy, openness, and relationship with my kids that I never dreamed was possible.

This newfound freedom gave me the courage to share snippets of my parenting struggles and failures online. I was scared because I knew I ran the risk of judgment and losing followers.

I've written about saving money for years on my blog, MoneySavingMom.com. Helping people find creative ways to cut costs, maximize the mileage of their money, and increase their income is my jam.

It's what I do. It's comfortable and safe for me.

Over the years, I've gotten used to people disagreeing with my take on credit cards or my stance on why I think everyone should consider using coupons. I'm even okay when people dislike my writing style or say that my blog is just not for them. But the thought of having people loudly criticize my parenting choices? That made me sick to my stomach.

However, in much the same way I felt compelled to share my money-saving methods for those who were desperately desiring to get in a better financial place, I couldn't help but also share what I was relearning as a mom and the resulting peace and joy I felt.

So, I timidly opened my virtual door and began letting you into my house, my family, and my life.

You walked in.

I saw what happened when I shared my struggles as a parent.

You walked in.

I saw what happened when I told you how much Jesus has changed the way my husband and I are raising our kids.

You walked in.

You showed up. You sat down at my kitchen table. You said you needed to know you weren't alone.

You started pouring out your own struggles and failures and stresses. You told me how tired you were of trying so hard. You confessed your anxiety over feeling that you were failing as a parent and didn't know what to do.

You confided your hopes and dreams for your kids. You bared your soul and shared your fear that you were messing it all up and doing it all wrong.

And so, I wrote this book for you.

On the pages ahead, you won't find a ten-step plan to raise obedient children or three strategies for effective discipline. What you will find are honest confessions and tried-and-true tactics I've learned for loving my kids more wholeheartedly.

I know parenting is a hot-button topic and everyone has strong opinions, so in the past I avoided most parenting-related questions by giving a response that went something like, "Ask me someday twenty-five years from now when my kids are all grown. I might have some answers then."

But when you showed up at my door and at my table, I felt an urgency to write the book now.

As I have opened up and given tiny glimpses into what God has been doing in my heart and life and in my approach to parenting, multitudes of moms and dads have asked me to share more.

I'm not a parenting expert or a psychologist. Nor am I writing this book because I've figured out the secret to producing perfectly parented offspring or because I feel I have all the answers. (Newsflash: I don't!)

I'm an everyday mom who is still very much actively parenting— I gave birth to baby number four while writing this book! I am right here in the trenches with you.

We have four biological kids, ages sixteen, thirteen, eleven, and eleven months (at the time this book is published). I'm also a foster mom, which means we often open our home to kids of various ages for a short stint or a longer period of time, depending on the needs. (In the middle of the first month of drafting this manuscript, we opened our home for a week to a ten-year-old girl who needed a place to stay while her foster family was out of town. A few weeks later, we accepted a long-term placement of a preemie baby who was in the neonatal intensive care unit [NICU]. More on that second placement in the last two chapters.)

This journey I've been on the past four years has changed my life from the inside out. And it's changed our home and our kids too.

I've stopped second-guessing myself so much and started focusing on leaning in and loving.

I've quit worrying constantly about my own reputation or what others will think and am resting and relying on God's still, small Voice of Truth to give me wisdom for the next step.

I've let go of thinking it all depends upon my doing it perfectly. I've realized that I will make mistakes and that it's better to openly acknowledge them to my husband and kids.

I'm believing the truth that I am uniquely equipped and chosen by God to be my kids' mom and Jesse's wife. That there is no one on the planet better suited for the task. My shortcomings and struggles will not ruin my kids or my husband. And I can trust God to fill in the gaps I leave.

I'm loving my kids and husband from a place of grace and a space of rest instead of a place of guilt and a space of stress.

It hurts me to see parents walking around with so much guilt, exhaustion, and feelings of failure and not-enough-ness. My heart in this book is to give moms and dads everywhere practical encouragement so you, too, can take steps toward parenting from a place of freedom and rest instead of burden and stress. Throughout these pages you will find not only my story and practical advice I've learned in my own parenting journey, but I also share tools and support to help you along your way. These include Scripture memory verses in bold, a manifesto or two, and at the end of each chapter, Two Transforming Truths for Love-Centered Parenting. Several other hands-on helps are compiled in the appendix—recommended readings, questions to foster better communication, a feelings chart, and Flare Prayers.

Are you ready to join me? Before we get started, here are two important notes:

1. **Don't freak out over the grammar!**

   Throughout this book you will notice that when I tell many stories, I use the pronoun *they* instead of *he* or *she*. The last thing I want to do in writing this book is to somehow hurt my kids' future or share stories that might cause others to view them in a negative light. Protecting my children is more important to me than following grammar rules.

Each of my kids has graciously agreed to allow me to use their stories in this book because they have seen the difference in a home shaped by love-centered parenting.

2. **This book was written for parents of younger children.**
I want to make it clear that I am not writing for parents of teens. Why? Because, y'all, I'm over here very much still parenting teens. And while I think many of the principles can apply to teenagers, I can't tell you how to parent teens because I'm still learning. There. I needed to get that off my chest. I didn't want you to think I believe I am qualified to advise you in this area when I haven't even raised a teenager to adulthood.

So this book is written for parents or grandparents of younger kids, or for those who don't have kids yet. It's the book I wish I had read when my kids were younger. It would have completely changed the way I parented in those younger years.

Okay, now that we've gotten all that out of the way, let's dive in to where this book all started . . . in the emergency room on one of the darkest days of my mothering.

# When You Don't Know What to Do

"My child is suicidal."

I could barely whisper the words to the woman at the emergency room desk when she asked why we were there.

My husband, Jesse, stood quietly behind me. We were both at our wits' end.

We had wrestled for days between feeling desperately overwhelmed one minute and resolute the next, pledging we would do whatever it took to help our child.

In just four weeks' time, our neat little life had shattered in pieces. All my parenting ideals were broken, and I was left reeling, scared, and devastated.

It all started one morning during drop-off at the little Christian school our kids were attending.

The day began in a normal way. The kids were excited. They had spent the morning chattering about their plans for the end of the school year and the field trip they were going on that day.

But then our normal day came to a halt when the principal stopped Jesse at drop-off and said he needed to meet with both of us and one of our kids after school.

We were caught off guard. Honestly, we had no clue what the meeting was about. Yet it was clear from the little the principal said that things were not okay.

All day we each felt a knot in the pit of our stomach. Our child had done something wrong, and we didn't know what it was. We racked our brains for any possible hint of anything being amiss the day before. Nothing came to mind.

We prayed. We tried to pass the time. And we had this ominous feeling that something terrible was about to go down.

We were right.

In the principal's office, we learned that our child had done something at school that broke the code of conduct and that swift action must be taken. We felt blindsided and in shock as the principal recounted what had happened.

But that was only the tip of the iceberg. Over the coming days, what we discovered would break our hearts in a million little pieces.

We knew that our child had struggled somewhat. I chalked it up to normal issues relating to friendships, growing up, and learning to get along. We had no clue that our child actually was deeply hurting and was taking out their hurt on others at school.

After our child was told they could not come back to the school, we uncovered many things that had happened in the last nine months. We found out that numerous parents had gone to the principal, telling him about issues between our child and theirs. Our child had been labeled a bully, and parents had been talking amongst themselves about our child's issues.

All this happened while we were completely oblivious. We naïvely assumed everything was going well. I had been on numerous field trips and attended weekly school functions with these parents. I had no idea they thought there were serious issues with our child and in our home.

I was at a loss as to how to help my child. As this all unfolded, our child began spiraling out of control. The simmering hatred and anger they had bottled up for months was spewing freely from their lips—and it terrified me.

Their anger at the world around them morphed into them saying things like "I should have never been born," or, "This world would be better off without me."

They became a shell of themselves, and I felt powerless to do anything about it.

At the same time, I had my own heart and hurts to try to sort out. On the one hand, I was angry and wounded that none of these parents had come to us to talk about any issues. I was also upset (and shocked, honestly) when I discovered that very negative things had been written about our child and posted online by parents—without any of them coming to me ahead of time to discuss what had happened.

I also felt stabbed in the back by parents with whom I thought I had a relationship. It hurt my heart to know they had been talking about me to others. And it cut deeply to have them now criticizing my parenting to my face.

One particularly low point occurred when I was meeting with another parent about my child and this whole situation. The other parent said something to the effect of, "I had thought your family was a Christian family with good morals. Clearly, some things are going on in your home that you aren't aware of for your child to be acting like this."

There was also a lot of shame bubbling up for me. I remember being sick to my stomach and feeling as though I was carrying around this crushing weight for days. How had I been blind to the fact that my child was struggling so much? And why did it seem everyone else's family was thriving while ours was falling apart?

*How had I been blind to the fact that my child was struggling so much? And why did it seem everyone else's family was thriving while ours was falling apart?*

I also experienced intense feelings of failure and guilt—especially when one parent looked me in the eye and said, "Our child never had issues until they met your child."

While I look back and realize that some of the accusations made toward us and our child during this time were unfounded and unkind, I also see how God used this as a huge wake-up call in my life.

Something did need to change. But what? And how had it come to this? Hadn't we done everything "right," just as our parents had with us?

My husband and I come from very conservative, God-fearing families. We both were homeschooled and raised in the church.

From an early age, our parents instilled God's Word in us. We read the Bible as a family almost every day, we prayed together daily (usually multiple times per day), we spent hours of our homeschool year studying Scripture, we memorized chapters and whole books of the Bible, we worked through a homeschool curriculum that was based on the Bible, and we were each encouraged to start our day with a personal quiet time reading God's Word.

We carried on this legacy and taught our kids about Jesus from birth. Actually, before birth. We were the overly ambitious parents who started praying and reading the Bible to our children in the womb!

In addition, we planned to protect our kids from worldly influences by homeschooling them through high school with the most Christ-centered curriculum we could find. Oh, and just to make sure we got a head start on this, we went to a homeschool conference when I was only a few months pregnant with our first child. Yes, you read that right. We could have won the award for homeschool parents of the youngest child in attendance, considering our student was still in utero!

Our vision for our family included having twelve kids, homeschooling them all, and being the poster family for godly parenting. I'm not exaggerating even a little bit here. We had lists of goals and dreams. We were highly motivated. And we thought we pretty much had all the answers.

I was so sure of my knowledge and wisdom that I wrote a pretty widely read blog called *Biblical Womanhood*. I taught women in great detail what you should and should not do if you were going to be a biblical woman. Did I mention that I was twenty-three years old, had only been married for two years, and had only one small child when I started this blog? Yep, I was so experienced that I needed to share my wisdom with the world (insert major eye roll here).

As you can probably guess, our life didn't quite pan out in the neatly packaged way we had planned. Yes, Jesse went to law school and we stayed out of debt (one of our first big goals). We had our first child (second goal). And he got the job he really, really wanted (third goal). And I got pregnant with our second child (woohoo, twelve kids, here we come!). But then things started unraveling when Jesse lost his job unexpectedly, soon after he was licensed as an attorney.

Around this time, my health also took a downward turn, and I was hospitalized for five days. They ran every test under the sun—or so it seemed—to try to figure out what was wrong. The doctors finally determined that my symptoms were the result of pregnancy-induced anemia and not something serious like leukemia, as they initially thought.

After our second baby was born, things went from bad to worse. Jesse couldn't find any work at all for three months, my health was still precarious, and our little church, which had been such a strong support to us over the last year, folded. We lost the one solid place of community we'd had since moving away from our family a few years before.

Our bank account was almost empty, we didn't have any steady income, we had a toddler and a newborn, and did I mention I was experiencing postpartum depression? We felt so alone, helpless, and scared.

> In the midst of the hopelessness, daily fear, and my terrible attitude, God was stripping away my pride, self-sufficiency, and legalistic view of the world.

In the middle of all of this, I began to question some of my staunchly held beliefs and convictions. I remember feeling so confused and discouraged. Why was God not giving Jesse a job? What were we going to do when the money ran out? Why was God not answering my prayers?

I took out the brunt of my fear and anxiety on Jesse.

I yelled at him pretty much every day. I was frustrated he couldn't get a job, stressed about how we were going to pay our rent and buy groceries, and so, so tired from caring for a newborn and toddler. I was also trying to keep up the facade of having it together for all the people reading my blog on how to be a biblical woman. Yep, I was still faithfully blogging there and pretending life was going along just fine!

Looking back, I see this season as a crucial turning point in my life. In the midst of the hopelessness, daily fear, and my terrible attitude, God was stripping away my pride, self-sufficiency, and legalistic view of the world.

When we got married, I remember thinking, *How on earth could anyone ever get a divorce?* And yet, on many of my worst days during this period, I didn't just yell at Jesse; I actually threatened to take the girls and leave him.

In hindsight, I realize how ridiculous this seems. When I needed him most, I was shoving him away and selfishly focusing on my own fears and worries. When he needed comfort and encouragement from me, I was offering the very opposite.

It humbles me to reflect on this time in our life and see how rocky and rough things were. It also moves me to have so much more compassion for others when they are going through hard times. I can no longer condemn or criticize another couple for having marriage struggles, because I have been there myself.

Walking through this dark season in our marriage forced me to take a good hard look at everything I believed. All my life, I had somewhat naïvely held to the conviction that if you honor God and make good choices, you will live a life of blessing.

But here we were, having honored God and made good choices, and we were falling apart. Where had we gone wrong? Why was this happening to us?

Slowly, ever so slowly, God began to reveal to me that I had put my faith and security where they should not be—in things other than Him: a job, a strong marriage, biblical choices, a good church and like-minded community.

My hope had been in earthly, temporal things that couldn't truly provide lasting hope.

A job couldn't save me.
A strong marriage couldn't save me.
A good church couldn't save me.
Even firmly adhering to biblical "rules" couldn't save me.
Only Jesus could save me.

I felt as if everything I had put my trust in was crumbling, and I had nowhere to turn but Jesus. I was so alone and scared. For days, I walked around in a daze. It felt as though the foundation I had stood on for so long had been ripped right out from underneath me. I was reexamining everything I had ever believed to be true.

I had nowhere to turn but to Jesus, and as I cried out to Him in desperation to provide for our practical needs, He did so much more than that.

In that place of feeling as though everything I had put my trust in was crumbling, God opened up my eyes to see how I had trusted in my good decisions instead of in God himself. My Christianity had been about doing everything right and following the rules instead of about having a relationship with Jesus.

As my loving and good Father (and the ultimate love-centered Father), He began transforming my heart to show me that I didn't need to rely upon my good works, my good choices, or a good life for my security. He was enough. He loves me. And I could rest in that.

**"See what kind of love the Father has given to us, that we should be called children of God; and so we are" (1 John 3:1).**

It would take years to undo and untether myself from my false beliefs that I needed to do more, be more, and strive harder in order to earn acceptance and love from the Lord. But little bit by little bit, I began to anchor myself to the belief that I was worthy of love not because of who I was or wasn't, but because of who God is and who I am in Christ.

---------

Nine years after that difficult year in our early marriage, our life looked very different than I ever expected it would. Instead of having a gaggle of kids, we had only three and hadn't been able to conceive again despite years of trying.

Instead of homeschooling all the way through high school, we'd felt God leading us to enroll our kids in a small private Christian school. Instead of being a full-time stay-at-home mom and running *Biblical Womanhood* on the side, I had long ago shut down that blog—no longer espousing most of the convictions and beliefs I had so strongly touted there—and was now the family's full-time breadwinner running MoneySavingMom .com.

True, my life hadn't panned out as I'd envisioned, but I was so fulfilled and felt we were truly seeking the Lord, honoring Him with our lives, and making wise decisions.

So how were we back in a place where everything was falling apart? Hadn't we sought the Lord at length about putting our kids in that tiny school instead of homeschooling? Weren't we trying to teach them about and point them to the Lord?

It felt like *déjà vu*, and I woke up every day with that familiar feeling of darkness, dread, and discouragement in the pit of my stomach again. I thought we had already been through this and learned what we were supposed to learn during that terribly rocky year of our marriage.

Why was this happening again, but this time with one of our kids? Were we just truly terrible parents? Had we completely missed the mark?

We didn't know what to do. A number of people suggested finding a counselor, and we decided to start there. Unfortunately, every counselor's office we called was either not accepting new clients or would not take our child. I remember calling one office that had been highly recommended to us and, after being asked several questions, I was told, "I'm sorry, we can't help you. It sounds like you need to hang up and go to the ER since your child is suicidal. We don't take kids who are struggling with those kinds of things." It was so frustrating! How were we supposed to get help for our child when even counselors wouldn't accept us?

Desperate and scared, we did as they told us. We packed up and went to the ER.

There, after they asked us and our child some questions, they whisked us into a room and made our child take all their clothes off and hand them over—including their shoes. We also had to have someone from the hospital in the room to monitor our child and us at all times.

While I understand that this was protocol, and I know the staff were just doing their best, it felt so painful and demoralizing as a parent.

As we all sat there waiting for hours, I descended to the lowest point I'd ever reached in my parenting. But it was there in the pit of despair that something beautiful happened:

God's love surrounded me and held me up.

It was that same feeling I'd had nine years earlier when I realized that so much of my life felt like it was crumbling around me, and yet God was there with me and He was enough. In that bleak hospital room, I felt His presence and knew that He was holding me and whispering, "I love you. I see you. I've not forgotten you. And I'm with you."

I sensed an overwhelming peace that He would carry me through. Little did I know how much I'd need that peace for the next year of intense counseling sessions, doctors' visits, receiving an official diagnosis with multiple letters and labels for our child, the hard road of figuring out the right medication and therapy, more doctors' visits, tests, and so many, many tears and prayers.

But we survived. True, we have some battle scars from that year, and things will never be the same again.

I'm okay with that.

And I'm here to tell you that God was with me through it all, and He has brought so much beauty from what felt like devastation. In fact, that heart-wrenching day in the principal's office started us on a journey to completely transform the way we approach parenting. Four years later, I'm a radically different mom and I have a totally different (and much better!) relationship with my kids.

That's why I wrote this book. I know that so many of you need a new way, when it feels like there's no way. Here's what I came to learn, and the truth that changed everything:

I realized that most of my parenting had been about me. I was parenting for my own approval and reputation instead of for my relationship with my kids and for their well-being. I cared more about what others thought than I did about my kids' hearts. I worried more about producing kids who made good decisions than about kids who knew they were wholeheartedly loved.

I parented from a place of stress and fear instead of from a place of rest and peace. I thought it was my job to bubble wrap and protect my kids from struggle and hurt. I was trying to be their

Savior and Holy Spirit instead of their nurturing, love-centered parent who pointed them to their Savior and gently led them to listen well to the voice of the Holy Spirit.

God allowed me to hit rock bottom so that He could help me relearn how to parent. But first, I'd need to let Him reparent me. I couldn't be a love-centered parent until I allowed myself to be parented by a love-centered Father God.

This book chronicles my journey. It's my story of letting go of control and manipulation and parenting for my reputation, and relearning to parent from a place of love and grace.

> *God allowed me to hit rock bottom so that He could help me relearn how to parent. But first, I'd need to let Him reparent me.*

I don't know where you're at in your parenting journey right now, but the fact that you picked up this book tells me your heart longs to deepen your relationship with your child.

Maybe you can relate to some of what I've shared above. Perhaps you have a child who is really struggling right now and you feel at your wits' end too.

Or maybe you picked up this book hoping you can prevent or protect your child from struggling. (Spoiler alert! As you'll read in subsequent pages, I think we do our kids more harm than good when we try to shelter them from experiencing anything hard in life. But I do think there are some amazing ways we can prepare them to better navigate and walk with them through tough situations. More on that later.)

You may have bought this book—or checked it out from the library—because you are curious about love-centered parenting and whether it works in the real world.

In the pages that follow, I am going to share the hard-won lessons, major changes, and entirely different approach to parenting I took as a result of that shocking visit to the principal's office.

It hasn't been an easy road, but it has changed our entire family in completely unexpected and beautiful ways. And I believe that these lessons and truths can transform your home too.

## TWO TRANSFORMING TRUTHS
### *for Love-Centered Parenting*

1. I can't be a love-centered parent until I allow myself to be parented by a love-centered Father God.
2. I don't have to rely on my good works or good choices for my security. Jesus is enough. He loves me. I can rest in that.

# This One Truth Will Change Your Parenting

When we came home from the ER that day, nothing was different. Our child was still struggling. I still woke up every morning feeling sick to my stomach and overwhelmed as soon as I opened my eyes.

We didn't have any answers. And we still felt so alone.

And yet, it felt like *everything* had changed.

The doctor who examined our child in the ER was so encouraging and kind. He decided that our child wasn't in any imminent danger, and we were able to go home with instructions to start counseling as soon as possible.

In addition, we had been given the name of a therapist who said she was willing to take us as clients. Having never been to therapy before, I had no idea what to expect. I felt apprehensive and embarrassed that it had come to this. Yet I also felt hopeful that maybe this could be the gateway to change for our child.

Before our child started their sessions, the therapist asked Jesse and me to come in for an initial session without our child.

I remember sitting on the couch in her office and telling her, "If you have any suggestions for how we can better parent our child, can you please let us know? Because I want to do everything I can to help this child."

Little did I dream that what the therapist would uncover had a whole lot less to do with my child's issues and would end up changing my entire approach to parenting.

In fact, after just a few sessions with our child, the therapist called me separately into the room and gently said, "I think you are trying so hard to fix and correct your child. What would it look like to just walk with them and love them instead?"

I remember sitting there wanting to defend my parenting choices. And yet, if I wanted something to change, something was going to have to change—and I needed to be willing to have that change begin with me.

Over the next few weeks, I paid close attention to how I parented and responded to my kids. I quickly realized that my go-to parenting style was correcting and overprotecting.

I began questioning where this approach to parenting came from. The more I asked myself, *Why are you responding like this?* the more I recognized that it was based upon years and years of believing lies about myself—personally, professionally, and as a parent.

These lies left a wake of destruction in their path and showed up in my daily internal dialogue as well as the words I spoke. Lies like

"I'm not good enough."

"I'm a disappointment to people."

"I'm just not cut out for this."

"I don't have what it takes."

"I'm failing."

"All the other moms seem to have figured out how to do this parenting thing well, and I'm a hot mess."

These negative words weren't flippant statements; I truly believed them to my core. They were the labels I wore. When I walked into a room, I would let them influence all aspects of my interactions.

For example, I believed the lie that most people simply tolerated me, but no one really liked me. As a result, for years I never allowed myself to trust people and I didn't believe I could be a good friend.

At other times, I let lies cloud my perception of myself as a parent. I felt like I was constantly failing, forever slipping up, and making a mess of my mothering. This led to intense guilt and beating myself up over my perceived shortcomings. I carried the weight of my failures around like baggage I couldn't put down.

At night, my fears and failures taunted me endlessly. I'd lie awake reviewing my day and think about how many times I had made mistakes. The heaviness of my lackluster parenting would eat at me and steal many hours of much-needed sleep.

But I assumed this level of guilt was normal. It was an unavoidable part of the parenting package, right?

Nope. As I've learned on my journey of transformation these past four years, I was dead wrong.

We can let go of lugging around our belief that we are inadequate.

We can say good-bye to the great weight of parenting guilt.

We don't have to suffocate under the stifling feelings of failure.

How do we do this? For me, my journey of transformation as a parent didn't happen as a result of a book I read or a chore chart I created or a seven-step strategy I implemented. It started by changing my core beliefs about who I was and what God thinks of me.

I had to dig down deep, uncover false beliefs, and uproot inner lies. And then I had to do what our pastor calls the "good, hard work" of changing what I believed from the inside out.

Often, when we pick up a parenting book, we're looking for a quick fix. We want to find the five-step plan to perfect parenting. Or the three-step solution to changing bad attitudes. Or the six strategies for overcoming anger.

Love-centered parenting isn't a short-term answer, quick-fix solution, or six-step strategy. It goes to the heart of everything you believe. It begins with the deep understanding that you are wholeheartedly loved by God and created on purpose for a purpose.

> You can't give what you don't have. You can't love your kids well if you don't believe you are fully loved yourself.

Because the truth is this: You can't give what you don't have. You can't love your kids well if you don't believe you are fully loved yourself.

Maybe you feel like you believe that already. If so, that is fantastic! But before you skip ahead to the next chapter, I'm going to ask you to stop and take an honest inventory of your heart and mind.

## Nixing the Negative Narrative

Think back over the last twenty-four hours. Have you said or thought any words that are negative toward yourself? What about the past seven days?

I'll give you a few examples:

"I need to lose fifteen pounds."

"I can't believe I bombed that presentation."

"I wish I could be more put together like her."

"Why does it seem like I just don't have the self-discipline that other people do?"

"Ugh, I failed yet again."

"It seems like I am forever dropping the ball."

"And of course . . . we're late yet again."

"This house is such a mess! Why are we the only family that lives like slobs?!"

"So much for all my great intentions! I can't seem to ever stick with any goal I set!"

"I hate how I look in this dress."

"I'm such a ditz."

"I wish I could just get my act together already."

You might not actually say these things out loud, but what are you telling yourself in your head? Is the narrative kind and encouraging or is it constantly putting yourself down?

Would you say the same words you say to yourself or about yourself to your kids or someone else you love?

A few years ago, I walked into the room to find my preteen daughter staring at herself in the mirror. She looked at me and the words tumbled out of her mouth: "I'm ugly."

When I heard her express this, my mama heart went into my throat. I wanted to simultaneously preach a lengthy sermon to her about how wrong she was, and also scoop her into my arms to reassure her that I think she is one of the most beautiful girls I've ever known—inside and out.

Instead, I heard myself utter some unexpected words: "You may not feel like you're beautiful right now, but the truth is that you are. I want you to know, you are welcome to voice how you're feeling (as in, 'I feel ugly') at any time. But I don't want you to make negative 'I am' statements about yourself, because they are actually lies, and we don't allow lying in our home."

Truth be told, I surprised myself with these words. As soon as I said them, I realized I needed to hear them just as much as she did. And it opened the door for us to have a heart-to-heart talk about how easy it is to believe lies instead of truth.

Just as I don't want myself or my kids to carry the weight of negative narratives, I don't want you to either. I have talked to so many parents in recent years who are carting around enormous guilt for the way they are parenting. They want to be kinder, more involved in their kids' lives, less irritable, more patient, more organized. They wish they could yell less, have a better routine, be more consistent.

Many parents pour out their hearts to me about how they constantly question the decisions they are making. Should they be more strict or less strict? Should they homeschool? Should they let their kids watch this or play that or eat this or that?

On the surface, their motives seem good. They love their kids and want the best for them. They want to raise their children the best way they know how.

But as I've had to learn on my own journey, so often at the root of this second-guessing and stressing over making the right decisions is a much deeper issue: believing the lie that we are ultimately in control of our kids' choices and futures.

It is no wonder parents are exhausted and feel so much guilt and pressure. They fear that if they don't get it right, their children are going to be permanently scarred for life.

They feel they need to parent as perfectly as possible and make the best decisions. This leads to the incessant feelings of failure and beating themselves up because, in their eyes, they are inevitably missing the mark.

I've got some amazing news for you today. You can stop striving for perfection. You can let go of feeling that you have to do everything right. You can lay down the heavy burden you're carrying and the weight of your child's future resting squarely on your shoulders.

Love-centered parenting is not about making all the right choices, doing everything perfectly, or never making mistakes. Love-centered parenting is about wholeheartedly loving our kids because we know how much we are wholeheartedly loved by God.

With this in mind, I'm going to make a bold statement: Many of our parenting struggles and feelings of failure can be directly correlated to our own false beliefs about ourselves and about God.

Our stress and guilt as parents—at the core—often are not because we have a difficult child, have made terrible choices, or aren't cut out for parenting, but because we don't understand the full truth of how much we are loved by God.

*Love-centered parenting is about wholeheartedly loving our kids because we know how much we are wholeheartedly loved by God.*

I love what Hayley Morgan says in her book *Preach to Yourself*:

Many of us—maybe all of us—don't live out what we say we believe. We live with broken, divided hearts if we don't allow God to continually hold us together. This is the cause of our dissonance— that strange suspicion that all of this isn't adding up.

This is why the songs of our lives aren't holding the same rhythm as the heart of God. We desperately want to believe these things, but our actions betray us.

- We say we depend on God, but we act like we've got to make it happen on our own.
- We say we believe God can heal, but we're walking around with decades-old wounds.
- We say we believe God is at work, but we're asleep at the wheel of this one life He's given us.[1]

If we say we believe we are loved wholeheartedly by God, why do we go around talking so negatively about ourselves? If we say we are forgiven, why do we continually beat ourselves up?

More than sixteen years ago, our first daughter, Kathrynne Elizabeth Paine, was born. We were over the moon. I could not imagine loving any person more than I loved this child. She was beautiful and absolutely the light of our lives.

I remember holding her in bed one morning while my husband was at law school. It was just the two of us, alone in our little basement apartment. I held her, looked into her eyes, and felt my heart might explode with love.

And then, I vividly recall feeling this overwhelming sense of understanding wash over me. I realized—for probably the first time ever—just how much I was loved by my heavenly Father.

I loved this precious baby girl in my arms more than words could express. And yet, my heavenly Father sees me in the very same light. He not only loves me as much as I loved my little girl, He loves me *more*. Because He is perfect, and His love is perfect.

"So that Christ may dwell in your hearts through faith—that you, being rooted and grounded in love, may have strength to comprehend with all the saints what is the breadth and length and height and depth, and to know the love of Christ that surpasses knowledge, that you may be filled with all the fullness of God" (Ephesians 3:17–19).

While that moment was a pivotal one for me, sadly, it took me ten more years to really begin to grasp at a heart level how much I was loved by God. And it wasn't until I truly and wholeheartedly believed how much I was loved by God that my parenting radically changed.

I'll say it again, because it bears repeating: Being a love-centered parent starts by believing the truth that we were created by a love-centered Father. Because you can't give what you don't have. If you don't believe you are wholeheartedly loved by the God of the Universe, you won't have a wellspring of love from which to pour out love to your kids.

This is one of the greatest parenting truths you'll ever encounter. And until you understand how deeply you are loved by your heavenly Father, you will not be able to love others deeply.

Psalm 103:11–13 says,

> For as high as the heavens are above the earth,
> so great is his steadfast love toward those who fear him;
> as far as the east is from the west,
> so far does he remove our transgressions from us.
> As a father shows compassion to his children,
> so the LORD shows compassion to those who fear him.

Stop and read those verses again.

Have you ever heard of the idea that through Christ your sins are removed as far as the east is from the west? Scripture clearly tells us this in these verses.

Take a minute and consider what this really means for us in the day-to-day. How would believing in God's steadfast love and immense compassion toward us change our lives? What would it look like to spend our lives camping on and resting in this truth?

Well, for me, it completely transformed my life—and my parenting!

## The Lies I Believed

As I stated earlier, for years I suffered from the destructive consequences of not understanding how much I was loved by God. Instead, I believed so many lies about myself.

These lies took root when I was a young girl. I'm not exactly sure when I started believing them. I do know that they originated from the father of lies—Satan himself—and they wreaked havoc on all areas of my life.

For the longest time, the words that I believed about myself were *Not enough*. I believed this lie long enough that it became my truth.

- I believed I wasn't good enough for friendship, so that's why I didn't have any close friends. To combat this, I became a world-class people pleaser. I spent years agonizing over whether people approved of me, and worked hard to win and keep approval.

- I believed I wasn't good enough when it came to school, so I tried to prove myself by becoming a workaholic and building a successful business. My hope was that this would show that I had worth and value. But I still felt like a big imposter.

- I believed I wasn't enough for my heavenly Father, so I worked hard to become the best Christian I could be, following a strict set of rules for what I wore, what I did and didn't do, what books I read, what kinds of movies I watched, who I associated with . . .

- I believed I wasn't doing enough as a parent. I would see all these other moms who seemed to be so much more put together, organized, and capable. I tried to make up for the shortcomings I felt I had by creating unrealistic and idealistic expectations for myself and my kids—which only produced enormous guilt and constant feelings of failure.

All of this made me feel like I needed to do better, try harder, strive more. I was inwardly miserable, constantly anxious, regularly struggling with panic attacks, incredibly lonely, and even suicidal.

I spent years of my life disappointed with myself. I felt deeply that I wasn't pretty enough, smart enough, funny enough, eloquent enough, confident enough, and on and on it went.

No matter what I did or didn't do, I'd be frustrated with myself that it wasn't enough.

I'd regularly think, *If only I were more this or that, then people would like me.*

I was my own worst critic for years, and I wholeheartedly believed the lie that I wasn't good enough.

As I learned the hard way, if you believe a lie long enough, you'll let it cloud everything in life—your relationships, your work, your parenting, and more.

*What you believe determines how you live.*

What you believe determines how you live, and these lies held me back from so much, including close friendships, business and ministry opportunities, and stepping outside my comfort zone. As a result, I lived in fear, guilt, insecurity, and shame, always feeling like I didn't measure up and was a perpetual failure.

## The Truth I Found

I vividly remember one day, while I was sitting in a worship service, it was as if someone whispered in my ear, "God thinks you're beautiful."

*He thinks I'm beautiful?* In the depths of my soul, I couldn't believe it.

In my mind, I was a misfit. I felt I wasn't the one you'd ever pick for anything. I felt I wasn't gifted. I felt I wasn't talented. I had struggled in school. I struggled to make friends and lasting relationships. I felt I was a disappointment to God and everyone else in my life. And I most definitely felt I wasn't beautiful.

But the seed of truth had been planted and I spent the next two years reading Scripture with new eyes and seeing what it had to say about who I am in Christ:

**"There is therefore now no condemnation for those who are in Christ Jesus" (Romans 8:1).**

"But now thus says the LORD, he who created you, O Jacob, he who formed you, O Israel: 'Fear not, for I have redeemed you; I have called you by name, you are mine'" (Isaiah 43:1).

**"But you are a chosen race, a royal priesthood, a holy nation, a people for his own possession, that you may proclaim the excellencies of him who called you out of darkness into his marvelous light" (1 Peter 2:9).**

"I have loved you with an everlasting love; therefore I have continued my faithfulness to you" (Jeremiah 31:3).

As I read these verses and many more, the seed of truth grew roots, and I began to believe deep down in my soul that He really and truly loved me—exactly as I was. I didn't have to do or be or strive or attain anything else to earn or win His love.

He sees me as covered in Christ's blood, and I am chosen, redeemed, loved, and accepted.

He thinks I'm beautiful.

When I truly believed this truth, it changed my whole world.

This gave me a completely new confidence. No matter what happens in life, no matter what people say, no matter whether someone likes me, I can stand in Christ—without condemnation. It doesn't matter what others think; I know who I am in Christ.

This truth rocked my world upside down! As Scripture says, "And you will know the truth, and the truth will set you free" (John 8:32).

I had been a Christian since I was twelve years old, but it wasn't until this revelation—years later—that I began to understand the fullness of the Gospel. It's not just about Jesus dying on the cross for my sins and eternal life in heaven. It's about so much more than that—it's hope and truth and freedom for each and every day of my life until I get to heaven.

He died on the cross so I can stop striving. When I put my faith in Him, I no longer have to try to be good enough. I am covered by the blood, and when God looks at me He sees Jesus.

I am loved. Accepted. Preapproved. I have incredible worth. In Christ. I am fully loved and chosen by the Creator of the Universe. And that is what defines me now.

Let me reiterate what I stated earlier: This understanding didn't happen overnight. It took a few years for me to really grasp and understand it, for it to sink in deep and permeate my very being.

And it required intentionality to get there. Here are three ways I committed to change my beliefs.

### 1. I started recognizing the lies.

Remember the conversation I had with my daughter about not saying "I *am* ugly"?

It might seem like a very slight difference in wording to say, "I *feel* ugly," versus saying, "I *am* ugly." But there is a stark contrast in what they communicate.

"I feel" is a statement of the genuine emotions I am experiencing in that moment. It could express things like

"I feel sad."

"I feel excited."

"I feel like I made a mistake."

"I feel lonely."

"I feel hopeful!"

On the flip side, "I am" statements could be truth (i.e., "I am a mom of four" or "I am a work-at-home mom"), or they could be lies we believe about ourselves, such as:

"I am a mistake."

"I am a disappointment."

"I am ugly."

"I am not enough."

There is a big difference between acknowledging that you *feel* something and believing that you *are* something.

The biggest transformation started for me when I began to identify the lies I was allowing to swirl around in my head. Statements such as "I don't measure up" and "No one likes me" were false beliefs I held about myself. Being able to recognize that these were actually lies, not truths, started me on the path to believing what God says is true about me.

### 2. I refused to believe the lies.

Psalm 139:14 says, "I praise you, for I am fearfully and wonderfully made. Wonderful are your works; my soul knows it very well."

When God created Adam and Eve, He saw His creation was "very good."[2]

God does not make garbage. God doesn't create worthless people. God didn't make people who are miserable mistakes.

> *There is a big difference between acknowledging that you feel something and believing that you are something.*

And yet, the false beliefs that I had repeated to myself for years said otherwise.

After I recognized how many false beliefs I was holding on to as truths, I made a commitment to take actionable steps to refuse to believe these lies. For me, this meant that every time a lie popped into my head about not being good enough or being a failure, I immediately made myself say, "That's a lie."

It might seem corny, but I challenged myself to say out loud, "That's a lie!"

There was something utterly life-impacting in naming these statements as lies instead of believing them and allowing them to taunt me as truths. It's as if they lost most of their power when I publicly declared them untrue.

### 3. I replaced the lies with the truth.

It was not enough to just recognize the lies and refuse to believe them. I had to take it one step further and replace these lies with truth.

I made myself speak phrases of truth any time I started hearing lies swirling in my head. If I thought, *I'm just not talented enough*, I'd immediately make myself say, "No, that's a lie." And then I replaced that lie with a truth.

So, in that case, I said something like, "I may not have the gifts that so-and-so does, but God has gifted me in other areas. He loves me just the way I am and wants me to embrace who He has made me to be instead of wishing I had different gifts and talents."

This simple act has transformed my thought life—and my *entire* life. It took a lot of work at first, but now it has become second nature to me. Not only that, but I also have a lot fewer lies swirling around in my head because I know and believe the truth in the core of my being.

Philippians 4:8 encourages this very thing: "Finally, brothers, whatever is true, whatever is honorable, whatever is just, whatever is pure, whatever is lovely, whatever is commendable, if there is any excellence, if there is anything worthy of praise, think about these things."

Fill your mind with truth, not lies! And guess what? There is scientific proof you can actually rewire your brain by doing this!

I was in the middle of writing this chapter when I picked up a copy of *The Whole-Brain Child*. These words jumped off the page at me:

> When we have a new experience or concentrate on something—say, on how we feel or a goal we'd like to achieve—that activates neural firing. In other words, neurons (our brain cells) spring into action. This neural firing leads to the production of proteins that enable new connections to be wired among the activated neurons. Remember, neurons that fire together wire together. This entire process—from

neural activation to neural growth and strengthened connections—is *neuroplasticity*. Essentially, it means that the brain itself is plastic, or changing, based on what we experience, and what we give our attention to. And these new neural connections, created when we pay attention to something, in turn alter the way we respond to and interact with our world. This is how practice can become a skill and how a state can become a trait, for good or for bad.[3]

The authors go on to say that "the physical architecture of the brain changes according to where we direct our attention and what we practice doing."[4]

What you think not only determines how you act, but it actually can rewire your brain! Cram truth—not lies—into your brain. Let that truth soak into your core and change your beliefs. Over time, as you begin to truly believe this truth, it will set you free! You will no longer live in shame, guilt, and insecurity but instead will be able to walk in confidence, fulfillment, and joy.

> *What you think not only determines how you act, but it actually can rewire your brain!*

It takes a conscious effort and is something you have to do over and over again. But if you commit to replacing lies with the truth every time they pop into your head, eventually it will become a habit. The lies will dissipate as you live under the truth.

Earlier, I referenced Hayley Morgan's book *Preach to Yourself*. I highly recommend reading this if you struggle with believing lies about yourself and about God. Here's another section of her book I have highlighted for myself and have read and reread:

> In order to best believe the good news, we need to clear the bad news out. The bad news I was believing when my spirituality was

lifeless was that God had forgiven me for my past but I was in charge of being perfect from here on out.

The bad news manifested itself in so many areas of my life.

I was worn-out from performing. And since I'd become so used to performing well, *everything* started to feel like a performance. It mattered more how my spiritual life appeared than how healthy it really was. And because I felt as though I was exhausting myself in trying to perform well, I was graceless with and annoyed at anyone else who didn't seem to be performing as well. Talk about no-good, bad-news antigospel, huh?[5]

Did you catch that? If we're not believing the truth of who we are in Christ, we are going to be constantly feeling the need to live up to an impossible standard of perfection. And there's a good chance we'll start expecting others around us to live up to this standard too (ahem, our kids).

It's incredibly encouraging to realize that I'm not the same woman I was a few years ago when we first had that heartbreaking and life-altering meeting with the principal and walked through such a dark time with our child. Little did I realize how much healing God was going to work in my own heart as a result of that devastating year.

Yes, I might still struggle with insecurity from time to time, but I feel much more healed and whole. I no longer see myself as a misfit who isn't good enough. Instead, I believe with all my heart that I'm beautiful in God's eyes. I know in the depths of my soul that He's created me for a specific purpose.

In Him, I'm whole, loved, and 100 percent enough.

I don't have to strive to be someone I'm not. I don't have to work hard to change my personality. I am enough in Him, exactly as I am.

This newfound confidence and wholeness has permeated all areas of my life. It has also inspired me to step outside my comfort zone and risk doing things I thought I would never do.

It has produced a depth of joy and more fulfillment in my life. It has given me courage to be authentic and vulnerable in relationships.

And it's completely changed my parenting. I can now parent from a place of knowing I am fully loved by God. He knows my heart and my desires. He knows my struggles and my shortcomings.

Have you ever stopped to consider the power of the last words Jesus uttered on the cross?

"It is finished."[6]

We don't have to try harder, do better, be more, do more, or strive more.

"It is finished."

We don't have to carry burdens that aren't ours to carry, try to be someone we weren't created to be, or work to earn God's favor.

"It is finished."

Jesus paid our debt in full. And when God looks at us, He sees Jesus.

This is the Gospel. This is the Good News.

And there is so much freedom, joy, and rest in this. We can love others wholeheartedly and live a life that glorifies our Maker—not because we have to, but because we get to.

## A Love-Centered Heart in Action

One of my kids was really frustrated over their grades recently. While I was trying to ask them questions to figure out the source of their frustration, they blurted out, "But I need to get all As!"

I stopped and quietly looked them in the eye and said, "Who put that on you?

"Where did the feeling that you need to get all As originate from? Is this something someone else is making you feel that you have to achieve?"

As we talked more, they admitted that it wasn't us (their parents), their siblings, a friend, or a teacher; it was their own self. They felt like they weren't measuring up to a standard they had set for themselves if they didn't get all As.

Parents, I think most of us have done the same. We've created a standard of perfection we feel we must achieve to be a great parent or to have a great kid. And if we're not hitting that self-made standard, we feel we are failing.

But who put that on you? While we might sometimes feel like there is pressure from outside sources, in most cases it's something we've put on ourselves.

And here's what I want to gently say to you: You don't need to carry that anymore.

Lay it down. Let it go.

The sooner you stop trying to live up to an impossible standard, the sooner you'll start experiencing deep joy and fulfillment in being okay right where you are.

Rest in Jesus. Rest in His finished work on the cross for you. Rest in the fact that He loves you more than you could ever fully comprehend. When God looks at you, He sees Jesus. In the next chapter, we'll talk about just how much this understanding can change your life. It profoundly changed mine!

## TWO TRANSFORMING TRUTHS
### *for Love-Centered Parenting*

1. I can't give what I don't have. I can't love my kids well if I don't believe I am fully loved myself.
2. Jesus finished the work on the cross so I don't have to be more, do more, strive more, or try harder. He loves me more than I can comprehend.

# Live as Loved

It was Presentation Day at school—the much-anticipated day when each child would get up and stand before the entire school (and packed seats of cheering parents and grandparents) and recite a poem or speech.

Silas chose a poetry recitation and we had spent weeks working on it together. In the days leading up to the presentation he quoted it flawlessly, and I knew he should have no issues reciting it in front of the auditorium full of people.

Dressed in his adorable little suit and tie, he walked up on stage . . . and then everything fell apart. He forgot part of the poem. He had to start over. As he walked off the stage, I could see the frustration and embarrassment on his face.

I went to him and whisked him into the lobby. I put my arms around him, looked into his eyes, and asked him how he was doing.

He started pouring out words. "Mine was the worst, Mom. I had the shortest poem and I forgot it. I'm going to get a bad grade. I can't believe I did that! I knew my poem so well!"

The failure he felt was palpable. I knew I couldn't change what happened on that stage just minutes before.

But there was one thing I could do: I could speak truth to him.

I told him that I was proud of him. I told him that having a good attitude and starting over again when you make mistakes is hard. And that it takes a lot of courage to begin again—especially when you've messed up in front of 150 people. I told him that he did his best—and that's all I care about. Jesse came over and echoed those same sentiments to him.

Within ten minutes, the shame was gone and a smile was in its place.

As I witnessed with my son and have seen so clearly in my own life, the truth sets us free—free to not live under the lies and labels or in shame and guilt.

Lies kill. Truth heals.

That might sound trite, but it's true. And while it's easy to say, it's much harder to actually let it sink in and change our lives from the inside out.

In the last chapter, I encouraged you to consider what lies you are believing and how they are wreaking havoc in your life, your marriage, your relationships, and your parenting. In this chapter, we're going to talk more about how to actually live out of the truth that you are fully and wholeheartedly loved by God.

Getting to the place of believing I was fully loved, forgiven, and accepted by God didn't happen overnight. Looking back, I can see a long string of events God used to slowly change my heart and my beliefs.

One of the first profoundly impactful parts of my journey came to me in the form of a message on Twitter.

Yes, Twitter. I don't even use the social media platform much anymore, but a number of years ago, I was pretty active on it and would often use it to send direct messages to people.

One day, after speaking at a conference, I was dialoguing with another one of the conference speakers via Twitter. I don't remember the details of what we were talking about, but the one thing that stands out is that at the end of our online conversation that day she wrote, "Live as loved."

Those three little words stopped me in my tracks.

Live as loved.

What did that even mean? What would it mean if I actually believed that and lived it out?

I tucked the phrase away and would often bring it back out and mull it over, thinking how much my heart longed for that to be my anthem.

I wanted this. I wanted to know what it would be like to believe I was loved and then live out of that love.

Fast-forward a few years, and God used another seemingly random occurrence to deeply impact me. It came from an episode of the *Trim Healthy Mama* podcast, of all places. (Trim Healthy Mama is a sustainable eating plan created by Serene Allison and Pearl Barratt, sisters from New Zealand who have quirky and lovable personalities.)

For a year or so, I loosely followed the Trim Healthy Mama eating plan, and I had gotten hooked on their podcast as a result. On one episode, they had Leah Thurber as a guest. I will never forget sitting in my car, listening to the podcast on my phone, and hearing her say,

"When you know you are so valuable and loved, there is a hiccup in your thought processes now . . . and you have a moment where you get to say, 'Whoa, whoa, wait a minute,' in relation to this situation, like, how am I going to see this now. . . . Remember, remember, I'm loved now, so how would Loved Me do this?"[1]

Podcast episodes are funny things to quote because they aren't all polished and put together, and often are more stream-of-consciousness expressions.

However, I didn't need her words to be perfectly crafted for them to hit me square in the forehead.

"How would Loved Me do this?"

She went on to describe how asking herself this simple question began to radically transform her heart.

I recall just sitting there and letting those words sink in.

"How would Loved Me do this?"

I started asking myself this as I went about life too.

When I went to that get-together where I knew almost no one, I asked myself, "How would Loved Me act?"

I realized that if I truly believed I was loved, I wouldn't worry about making a good first impression or how I was perceived. I would just focus on others, reach out and ask questions, be friendly and warm, and wholeheartedly love others well.

So that's what I did, because I am wholeheartedly loved.

When I walked into an awkward meeting that I was dreading, I asked myself, "How would Loved Me act?"

Loved Me would stop stressing over saying things perfectly, making sure people liked me, or psychoanalyzing other people's responses. I would just show up as myself and confidently love others well.

So that's what I did, because I am wholeheartedly loved.

When I faced a critical comment from someone about a choice I had made, I asked myself, "How would Loved Me respond?"

I knew Loved Me wouldn't be upset, beat myself up, or feel defensive. Instead, I would listen to hear if there was any truth I needed to receive (and get counsel from others if I wasn't sure), and then receive it and take it to heart. If there wasn't any truth I needed to hear, I could let it go.

So that's what I did, because I am wholeheartedly loved.

When my kids were arguing amongst themselves and saying unkind words, I asked myself, "How would Loved Me respond?"

Not by feeling frustrated at myself that I apparently had dropped the ball in parenting my kid or snapping at my kids with angry words like, "I expect better from you!" Or worse, yelling at them for yelling—anyone else been a hypocrite like that before? Loved Me would stop, take a deep breath, and calmly address the situation.

So that's what I did, because I am wholeheartedly loved.

When someone came to me to express disapproval in a choice one of my kids made, I asked myself, "What would Loved Me do?"

Loved Me wouldn't feel the need to be defensive, hurt, or angry. Loved Me could listen and receive the words of disapproval and not take them as an indictment on my child, myself, or my parenting. Loved Me would believe that the person was doing it out of love for me and my child, regardless of how the message was delivered. I could then address the issue with my child, if it needed to be addressed, or let it go, if it was something that could be let go.

*"What would Loved Me do?"*

So that's what I did, because I am wholeheartedly loved.

See how this one simple question can completely change the way you approach so many situations in life?

How would it change your life to not only believe you are loved, but to take the next step and live as loved? What would you do differently than you are doing now? How would you interact with others differently? How would you parent differently?

Jeannie Cunnion shared a word from her book *Mom Set Free* on her Instagram a few years ago that stopped me in my tracks: "The grace we soak in is the grace that seeps out."[2]

We sing about amazing grace, but rarely do we let it soak into our hearts so that we are overflowing with it and can't help but share it with others—especially our kids.

If we're not soaking in grace, we won't have grace to give out.

It's the same way with love. If we're not soaking in love from our heavenly Father, we won't have a reservoir of love to share with others.

In my teenage years, I read multiple books by and about Amy Carmichael. She was a brave single woman who went to Calcutta, India, to serve as a missionary.

In addition to rescuing many girls from being sex slaves in the temple and then mothering them in the orphanage she ran, Carmichael also was an avid writer. In her lifetime, she penned many words now collected in published volumes.

Many of her quotes will forever impact who I am as a person, but one I often come back to is this one: "For a cup brimful of sweet water cannot spill even one drop of bitter water, however suddenly jolted."[3]

Did you catch that? If you have a cup filled with sweet water (or your favorite sweet beverage—I'll take a yummy decaf chai tea latte myself) and you bump it, the only thing that's going to spill out of it is the sweet beverage.

Bitter water or some other nasty drink can't come out of a cup filled with sweet water (or chai tea latte), because that's not what's in it.

The same is true in our own lives. If we are filled up with the knowledge of how much we are loved by God, when we are bumped, poked, or prodded by others or by situations, only kindness, love, and truth can slosh out of us.

To put it another way, think about a dry sponge. It's going to soak up whatever comes in its path—whether that is sweet water or bitter water (truth or lies). But if a sponge is completely sopping wet, it can't really soak up anything else.

My goal is to soak up so much truth in my everyday life that there isn't any space for lies to take up residence in my mind and heart.

## Fill Yourself Up with Truth

If we want truth and love to seep out of us, we need to immerse ourselves in them. Here are some practical ways to do so:

- Listen to uplifting music that speaks of the goodness of God.
- Read books or listen to audiobooks (I love using the free Libby app!) that fill your mind with the truth.
- Have the lock screen on your phone show a verse or visual reminder of truth.
- Write Scriptures on your mirror with dry erase markers.
- Send reminders of truth in texts or short notes (yes, the kind you actually write by hand and mail) to your friends.
- Post words of truth on your walls.
- Pay attention to the words you are speaking to yourself and replace the lies with truth, as we addressed in the last chapter.
- Memorize Scriptures that remind you of the truth of who you are in Christ. (See the Memory Verse cards on

pages 215–219.) Read these every morning when you get up and again before you go to bed.

- Get a pad of AquaNotes waterproof shower notes, available from Amazon, and write out words of truth for your shower walls.
- Put words of truth on your fridge or above your kitchen sink.
- Speak words of truth to your kids. Consider having a particular verse or truth reminder that you say in the mornings together at breakfast, before they leave for school, while they are brushing their teeth or you're changing their diapers or giving them a bath, or before you eat dinner.

Guess what else happens when we drench ourselves in the truth? We don't have as much time to dwell on the lies!

You know what also results? The atmosphere in our home can dramatically change.

As parents, we set the tone of our home. When Mom and Dad fully believe they are loved by God and they live out of that love, there is going to be so much more calmness, peace, warmth, and kindness in your home.

Monte Swan poignantly states in his book *Romancing Your Child's Heart*, "The atmosphere in a home originates in the hearts of parents."[4]

I have the privilege of co-leading a small group of high school girls in our church youth group. Recently, our youth pastor was preaching about how believing the Gospel and how much we are loved by God will change our life.

As I sat in my row that Wednesday night, surrounded by these high school girls who are so special to me, I couldn't help but think about how I wished I had known this truth when I was younger.

Yes, I grew up in church. Yes, I heard the Gospel more times than I can count. Yes, I believed in God and Jesus and the Holy Spirit.

But I held that belief in one hand while I held on to my lies that I wasn't enough with the other. And that's why I struggled so much, felt ongoing anxiety, and worked so hard to do the right thing. It was a constant tug-of-war between the lies and the truth. You can't believe both at the same time.

I thought I had to earn God's love. And I did so by pursuing holiness and living a righteous life.

But this life never satisfied me. It was never enough, because I never believed I was enough.

As our youth pastor read 1 Peter 2:9 from *The Message*, I literally wanted to stand up and tell all of the young people in the room, "Listen up! Don't miss this! Really and truly. Listen and let this truth permeate the depths of your soul."

Stop and read what this verse says: "But you are the ones chosen by God, chosen for the high calling of priestly work, chosen to be a holy people, God's instruments to do his work and speak out for him, to tell others of the night-and-day difference he made for you—from nothing to something, from rejected to accepted" (1 Peter 2:9 MESSAGE).

I could see myself maybe even standing up on my chair in the sanctuary at this point and getting really passionate as my voice grew louder and stronger and I said, "Hear me out! I don't want you to have to spend years wandering around in insecurity and wondering if you are enough. GRAB HOLD OF THIS TRUTH NOW, WHILE YOU'RE YOUNG! THIS WILL CHANGE YOUR LIFE!"

Okay, so I didn't stand up and make a spectacle of myself by saying all that, but I did read the words of this verse over and over again to myself—and then read them aloud to the girls during our small group time!

You are chosen by God. You are God's instrument to do His work. He has created and gifted you in unique and special ways.

You don't need to try more, be more, or do more. You don't need to work harder, aim higher, and perform better.

You are enough in Him.

And He loves you more than you can ever dream or imagine. It's this love that will make a night-and-day difference in your life.

He has fully loved you and accepted you. You are preapproved in Him.

When He looks at you, He sees a masterpiece. He sees His child. He sees His deeply loved creation.

Even on the dark, discouraging, difficult, and downright awful days, we are still fully and completely loved by God. How would it change your life to truly believe this?

**"Who shall separate us from the love of Christ? Shall tribulation, or distress, or persecution, or famine, or nakedness, or danger, or sword? As it is written, 'For your sake we are being killed all the day long; we are regarded as sheep to be slaughtered.' No, in all these things we are more than conquerors through him who loved us. For I am sure that neither death nor life, nor angels nor rulers, nor things present nor things to come, nor powers, nor height nor depth, nor anything else in all creation, will be able to separate us from the love of God in Christ Jesus our Lord"** (Romans 8:35–39).

Nothing can separate you from God's love. Absolutely nothing. Do you believe that? Are you living like you believe it?

Becky Keife penned it so perfectly in her book, *No Better Mom for the Job*:

> Nothing can build a wall between you and God's love. Nothing can disqualify you from receiving it. Not your son's finicky temperament or your daughter's wild expressiveness. Not your fatigue or embarrassment as a result of the craziness. When you make the wrong call, go to battle with your kids over something that doesn't really matter, when you're inconsistent or overlook something that was actually important, when you under-prepare or overreact, God loves you no more and no less.
>
> In other words, the world's forces, our kid's choices, and our own crud cannot sever us from God's love.
>
> Yesterday, today, and tomorrow. To the moon and back. He loves you.[5]

Let this truth soak deep into your heart. Let it change your life. And let it change your parenting.

Because here's the thing: You have the opportunity to show Christ's love to your kids every single day. You get to represent Jesus on a daily basis.

And in the process, you get to teach them the truth of how much they are loved by God.

*The most impactful way you can help your kids understand God's love is for them to see it lived out in your life on a day-to-day basis.*

I challenge you to do more than read verses to your kids about how much God loves them or to sing songs about God's love or to just say, "God loves you."

The most impactful way you can help your kids understand God's love is for them to see it lived out in your life on a day-to-day basis. They need to see you walking in the truth and letting that truth seep out of you into all of your actions and interactions.

---------

Kathrynne started taking an art class at school the semester before I began writing this book. She had sketched some in the past, but it had been a while. So we were all surprised when she started bringing home these really impressive art pieces she did at school. What shocked us even more was how much she was loving it. She began sketching all sorts of things at all hours of the day and night—just for fun.

You need to understand that she's not the typical creative, artsy type. She's very athletic and a math whiz. But art? Well, it just wasn't something we ever thought would be her thing.

However, we've worked hard not to box our kids into a stereotypical label, and I'm all for them having a plethora of interests and passions—even if they seem widely varying or unexpected.

On a recent day off from school, I watched her spend hours meticulously working on a drawing. When she was done, she showed me the finished picture, and I told her how amazing it was.

"Really? You think it's good?" she asked.

She pointed out the flaws and mistakes and things she wished she had drawn differently. I didn't see any of that; I saw a masterpiece that she had worked so diligently on, using her gifts and talents in a beautiful way.

I couldn't help but think how often we're like this. We focus on our mistakes, our shortcomings, and what we wish we had done differently . . . when our heavenly Father sees something else entirely.

He sees our heart. He sees our diligence. He sees our effort. He sees the investments we are making when no one else is watching.

He sees our tears and our struggles. He sees our shortcomings, but He doesn't judge us by those. When He looks at us, He sees beauty. He sees a masterpiece.

**"For we are God's masterpiece. He has created us anew in Christ Jesus, so we can do the good things he planned for us long ago" (Ephesians 2:10 NLT).**

Yes, you right there. You, who might be feeling like you just don't have what it takes and you will never measure up. Yes, you. He sees you as a masterpiece in Christ.

You, who might feel like you're failing and falling short. Yes, you. You are His masterpiece.

When we rest in that understanding of how much He loves us and how He views us, we can stop trying to find that love and fulfillment in other things and people—including our kids.

Last night, I hosted a group of ladies from church at our house. Over hot mugs of tea and the most delicious Trader Joe's chocolates, we talked about how we so often seek our fulfillment in many things and people and activities and places outside of God alone. At first glance, these things might seem good. And most of them are, as long as they aren't taking the place of God.

- It's a good thing to want deep fellowship and community with friends. But it becomes idolatry when we need that and pursue that more than we need and pursue God.

- It's a good thing to want to make a difference in the world and use our gifts and skills to impact others. But it becomes idolatry when we find our joy and life in being recognized, being significant, or making a difference.

- It's a good thing to want to have a strong, vibrant relationship with our spouse. But it becomes idolatry when we are dependent upon their love and need that love to feel happy and fulfilled.

- It's a good thing to want to raise kids who have strong character, who love Jesus, and who are emotionally and spiritually healthy. But it becomes idolatry when we need those outcomes in order to be happy and hopeful and fulfilled.

When we look to anything apart from Jesus to find our life and joy, we are missing the mark.

One of the women made the analogy of how we are like desperately dehydrated people who carry around our IV poles trying to hook up to things and people to try to fill our veins with approval, admiration, and affirmation.

I know I've done this so many times! A simple way to do a heart check on whether or not we are seeking to find life outside of Jesus is by paying attention to what we pay attention to. Where are our thoughts automatically going when we're not actively engaged in something else?

For instance, what do you think about when you're driving or showering? What does your mind go to without being prompted?

Are you stressing over something? Psychoanalyzing a recent conversation and feeling that you failed or said the wrong thing? Making up stories about a situation when you don't know all the facts? (I love the way Brené Brown puts it in *Rising Strong*: "In the absence of data, we will always make up stories.")[6]

Let's put this in the context of parenting. Think back to the last few weeks. How often did you:

- Beat yourself up for how you handled a situation with your kids?

- Feel like you didn't parent well enough?
- Struggle with guilt that you're not doing enough for your kids or spending enough time with them?
- Stress over whether you were making the right decisions for your child?
- Worry about decisions your child is making?
- Compare yourself to other parents or compare your kids to other kids?

Any time we are worrying, stressing, beating ourselves up, or comparing, it's a clear indication that we're not resting in how much we are fully loved by God. Instead, we are trying to take control, be our child's rescuer, or thinking that our child's current and future success is entirely dependent upon us.

Attempting to control, fix, save, and/or micromanage our child's life and future is a recipe for constantly feeling overwhelmed, stressed, and guilt-ridden. Instead, Jesus is asking us to open our clenched fists and rest in how much we are loved by Him. It's in this place of resting and soaking in His love for us that we can wholeheartedly love our kids.

*It's in this place of resting and soaking in His love for us that we can wholeheartedly love our kids.*

You might be shaking your head right now, feeling frustrated because letting go of control and resting in God's love sounds so simple and yet so scary.

Let me shoot straight: It is simple, but it's also one of the hardest things I've ever done. It has meant taking several steps, daily, that I have crafted into the following manifesto to help you begin to live as loved too.

# LIVE LOVED MANIFESTO

Today, I commit to live as loved. I choose to believe I am fully and wholeheartedly loved by God for exactly who I am. I don't have to be more, do more, or achieve more to be loved by Him.

When I am tempted to believe the lies that have held me back for so many years, I will replace those lies with the truth that I am fully loved by God.

Jesus loves me unconditionally and doesn't judge me based upon my kids' behaviors or choices. I will put my hope in Him, not in my child's choices. I choose to be okay with my children making mistakes and messing up because I know this is why Jesus came.

I will focus on pointing my kids to Jesus and will no longer spend my days trying to be my children's rescuer and Holy Spirit.

I choose to open my tightly clenched fists trying to control all of life, and hold out my hands to accept the gift of God's love for me.

I refuse to believe the lies that tell me I'm not measuring up and am missing the mark of perfection as a parent. Instead, I choose to rest in the truth that I am created in the image of God and He sees me as His masterpiece. I don't have to beat myself up when I feel like I don't have what it takes but will remember that I am enough in Christ.

I was made for more than living a life stifled by lies and suffocated by false beliefs. I will replace those lies with the truth of who I am in Christ.

I am loved. I am forgiven. I am enough in Christ.

Jesus, thank You for loving me exactly as I am. Thank You for not expecting me to parent perfectly, but for being the Ultimate Example of a Love-Centered Parent to me.

I rest in Your amazing love for me. Let me be a conduit of God's love to others. May it pour through me and spill out to everyone I come into contact with.

I don't know your story. I don't know the pain, the hurt, the struggles, the loss, or the grief you've walked through.

I don't know what others have said about you or done to you or taken from you.

I don't know the burdens you are bearing right now or the heaviness that might be deep in the pit of your stomach as you are reading these words.

But I do know this: In Christ, you are enough.

In Christ, you are forgiven, chosen, loved, and accepted.

When He sees you, He sees a masterpiece.

You are loved. Live as loved.

Ask yourself: How would Loved Me live?

## TWO TRANSFORMING TRUTHS
### *for Love-Centered Parenting*

1. I am God's masterpiece, made in His image for His glory and purpose.
2. I am fully and wholeheartedly loved by my Creator God. Knowing this and believing this allows me to live as loved.

# Your Job as a Parent

A s I was cleaning up the kitchen one morning, I came across a stack of papers on the countertop. I flipped through them to see what they were, and my eyes landed on a note one of my kids had written to a friend.

I quickly glanced through the note and then I saw it: In the middle of a sweet letter, there was a crass word. And I immediately wanted to flip out.

My brain went into worst-case scenario mode and I thought, *What if my child uses this kind of language at school and around friends and just pretends to be a person of integrity at home?* I went so far as to think, *Is my child leading a double life?*

I know it sounds crazy, but I am guessing you may have had moments like this too. Moments when you can take a small infraction on the part of your child and blow it up into mammoth proportions.

My mind began spiraling out of control. I felt part panicky and part sick. And I almost threw all my calm and controlled parenting out the window. I felt the fear and frustration rising in me and I wanted to go into full-on freak-out mode, sternly call my child into the kitchen, and launch into a passionate sermon about how they should "NOT ever say that word!!"

Four years ago, that is exactly what I would have done. I would have heatedly spewed words to my child about their language, and probably would have hurt them by saying shaming things like, "You should know better than to say terrible words like that!" Oh, the irony.

But that day in the kitchen, instead of letting out a tirade of wounding words, I heard the Holy Spirit quietly reminding me of one of my mothering mantras: "Lean in and love."

I called my child into the kitchen and said gently, "Can we talk about this letter you wrote? I thought it was so nice, but I was a little concerned about this one word you included."

They looked confused. And then it hit me: They didn't even know it was an inappropriate word! As we talked more, I realized that this child had heard some adults say this word and just assumed it meant something that it didn't mean.

We were able to have a heart-to-heart conversation about the connotations of this word and why it's derogatory. We also talked about not repeating a word that you don't understand simply because you've heard an adult in your life use it. Unfortunately, just because an adult in authority says it, that doesn't necessarily mean it's an appropriate word to use.

After we finished this conversation, I immediately stopped to thank the Lord for how He is working in me as a mom. I'm especially grateful He is helping me to think before I react, and to ask more questions and preach fewer sermons.

Most of all, I am so grateful for how parenting from a place of leaning into my heavenly Father's love is spilling out into the way I parent and interact with my kids.

In the previous chapters, I shared the deep work God did to transform my heart from believing I wasn't enough, to believing and living out the truth that I was fully loved by the God of the Universe. In this chapter, I want to unpack how that has changed the way I love my kids. I also want to give you some practical examples of how this can look in everyday life.

- - - - - - - -

Note: If you're anything like me, there's a chance you may have skimmed the last few chapters and then skipped ahead to this one because you are ready to dive into the practical application. Can I encourage you to take the time to go back and thoroughly read the previous chapters? Not only are they important, but they are the foundation upon which all of these practical principles rest.

If you try to implement the strategies I'm going to share without a fundamental understanding of your heavenly Father's love for you, you'll likely end up feeling frustrated and exhausted. It will be like trying to put a bunch of bandages on a broken bone. Until you reset the bone (if needed) and cast it, it won't heal properly. In the same way, your heart and your deep understanding of your identity need to be in line or you won't be in a place to wholeheartedly love your kids.

## Why We're So Exhausted and Stressed as Parents

While I was writing this chapter, I asked on my Instagram Stories for people to finish this sentence: "My job as a parent is to _____."

There were hundreds of responses. I noticed right away that very few of them focused on things that we have any control over as a parent.

The majority of the responses were along the lines of:

- My job as a parent is to raise responsible, independent adults.
- My job as a parent is to raise godly children who love Jesus with all their hearts.
- My job as a parent is to raise kids who make good choices and are people with good morals and character.

Now, please hear me out: None of those are bad aspirations. In fact, I hope my kids grow up to love the Lord, love others, and have great character.

However, I can't control the outcome or the results of my parenting. Only God can change someone's heart. My kids' choices, behavior, morals, and character are ultimately not something I am fully in charge of.

*I can't control the outcome or the results of my parenting.*

Yes, I can lead them and guide them and (hopefully) set a good example for them. But at the end of the day, their choices and actions and attitudes are theirs to own.

As I read response after response to my Instagram question, my heart felt burdened for these well-meaning parents. They wrote in and talked about the weight they feel to get it right, to help their kids turn out well, and to raise responsible adults. They shared how overwhelmed and frustrated they are that it feels like their best efforts aren't working.

If you believe it's your job as a parent to raise responsible kids or to raise kids who love Jesus or to raise kids who make good choices, your job performance as a parent is based solely upon how your kids turn out. Not only is this a crushing load to carry, but it will cause you to be hypercritical of your kids' choices because you feel like they directly reflect on your parenting. (This belief will also likely make you highly critical of other parents and their kids' behaviors too.)

Moms and dads, I have good news for you! Your success or failure as a parent is not based on how your kids turn out and the choices they make!

That might sound very counterintuitive to everything you've ever believed and the way you've always parented. In the chapters that follow, I'm going to present you with a different way to parent—one that is based on love, not perfection, and relationship-building, not performance. Later in this chapter, I'll give you a peek at what that entails and what your job actually is as a parent.

But first, I think we need to talk more about what is not your job as a parent. There are many misconceptions floating around— thanks to the internet and our own inner critic—as to what we need to be as parents. Most of these are dead wrong.

## Our Job Is Not to Be Perfect Parents

I know you've probably heard this again and again. In fact, there's currently a strong "authenticity" trend online where it's almost hip to show how much of a hot mess you are.

Sure, we can say with our lips (or our little Instagram photo texts) that we need to "let go of perfectionism" and show up as our real selves, but it's a lot harder to actually follow through with this philosophy. Well, let me rephrase that. It's not hard to be imperfect, but it's hard to truly let go of the pursuit of perfection.

Let's take a little pop quiz. Have you ever:

- compared yourself with another parent?
- felt like you really don't measure up as a parent?
- beaten yourself up for feeling like you failed your kids?
- felt stress and anxiety over whether you are doing enough as a parent?

When we're doing any of those things, it's an indication that we're likely holding ourselves to a pretty high standard. Okay, it might not be a perfect standard, but it might give perfect a run for its money!

Instead of parents who are pursuing perfection, our kids need parents who are humble enough to admit when they've made a mistake, missed the mark, and messed up. That is going to speak louder to kids than parents who are so focused on perfection that they lose sight of the big picture!

> *Instead of parents who are pursuing perfection, our kids need parents who are humble enough to admit when they've made a mistake, missed the mark, and messed up.*

Do you know what else can happen when we pursue perfection? We miss out on being present.

A year or so ago, I was at a conference with a couple who were expecting their first child. They had been trying and hoping for years to have a baby, and she was telling me about their difficult journey to getting pregnant. I looked at her baby bump and remarked, "I can only imagine how excited you must be, thinking about having a baby after waiting and praying and hoping this would happen for so long!"

Her response caught me completely off guard. "Actually, I've been more focused on researching all the things I need to know after the baby gets here. I'm stressed thinking about what things we need to buy and what we're going to do about vaccinations."

I wanted to take her by the shoulders and gently but firmly say, "You're having a BABY! You've waited years for this!!"

Since I didn't know her well, I restrained myself from being so forthright. But it was such a good reminder of how we often are so intent on doing things right, making the right choices, doing the research, and then stressing or overanalyzing our decisions that we miss out on the blessings and beauty and gifts right in front of us.

I say this because I've been there. I always want to be a Present Moment Mama. But I have missed out on many present moments because of a laser-intense focus on the future.

Instead of sitting and soaking up the sweetness of having a little baby, I've been distracted by guilt over not having my child on a better schedule and thinking about what I need to change or tweak. When I could have been enjoying a special conversation with a toddler who was just learning to communicate, I was instead wrapped up in an internal dialogue and feeling discouraged that I couldn't be more organized and creative like so many other moms.

I've wasted hours and hours of time, lost sleep, and beat myself up over so many silly things over the years—like the week that I struggled to go to sleep multiple nights because I had discovered my kids weren't brushing their teeth three times a day and I worried that they were all going to get a dozen cavities or worse! I've let fear of the future and fear of failure steal my joy and delight in the present.

## Our Job Is Not to Overprotect Our Kids

As a parent, one of my roles when my kids are little is to protect them, to make sure they stay safe and out of danger. They don't know that a stove is hot and can burn them, that walking onto a street where cars are driving is dangerous, that jumping off a five-foot wall could hurt them, and that it's not okay to drink the bathroom cleaner.

It is my responsibility to help teach them these things, to help them be aware of danger, and to instill a healthy fear of potentially hazardous situations in them.

As they've gotten older, I've realized that my role needs to shift. While I want to bubble wrap my kids and keep them safe and make sure they never struggle or face hard things, I know deep down that's not preparing them well for life.

As Jesse wisely said on one of our podcast episodes, "Struggle builds strength." If I always protect my kids from heartache and hurt, I'm doing them a disservice. I'm teaching them to be weak and wimpy, and I'm raising them to be children who rely on their mom instead of adults who rely on God.

I don't want to see my kids fail, but I know that letting them try new things, mess up, or experience failure will help them develop character that success never will.

I don't want to see them get hurt by others, and yet if I swoop in and rescue them from every hurtful situation, they'll never learn how to work through disagreements, have difficult conversations, stand up for themselves, and love people who are challenging to love.

I don't want them to make mistakes, and yet I know that some of my greatest life lessons have been the result of mistakes I've made.

It's so tempting to spend our days as parents trying to save our kids from hard things, but our job is not to be our kids' rescuer but to point them to Jesus. We can set an example and teach them right from wrong, but we can't ultimately make them do the right thing or make the God-honoring choice—especially as they get older.

As someone who grew up in a very conservative homeschooling community, I watched many parents work hard to protect their kids from what they considered "worldly." They would remove all outside influences—including music, movies, books, and relationships they felt were inappropriate. Some went so far as to get rid of the television altogether, just to make sure their kids weren't exposed to anything ungodly.

There were rules for what kids could wear, watch, and listen to. There were strict guidelines for who kids could associate with and where they could go—even when they were in their late teens or older.

I know that the heart behind this (in most situations) was the parents' desire to raise godly kids. In addition, I know they (almost always) wanted what was best for their kids and were trying to do the right thing. Yet in so many cases, I saw it produce rebellion and broken relationships with parents.

I also have witnessed many of these very protected kids swing the pendulum far, far to the other side once they were no longer living at home. Many have completely rejected Christianity, and some have even cut off their relationship with their parents.

Here's what I have learned from years of observing this pattern: We can put as many safeguards and protections in place as possible, but these will not change our child's heart. Yes, a child might adhere to the rules and follow the guidelines outwardly, but they could be seething with rebellion and anger on the inside.

As we talked about in an earlier chapter, only Jesus can save us and set us free. **"So if the Son sets you free, you will be free indeed"** (John 8:36).

Outward performance is not necessarily a direct indication of inward change. Strict rules and rigidity will never save a child, a preteen, a teen, or even an adult. They might prevent someone from consequences at times, but they will never change someone's heart.

*We can put as many safeguards and protections in place as possible, but these will not change our child's heart.*

This is why I believe there can be great danger in overprotecting our kids. Doing so not only fails to prepare them for the real world—where temptation, hurt, and hard things abound—but it also can keep them from building up their own convictions, backbone, and character.

## Parenting Is Not a Project

In addition to falling prey to pursuing perfection or overprotecting our kids, we are also often tempted to approach parenting as we would a task or project. We want to define our end objective, break down the steps we need to take to get there, and expect that there will be regular mile markers of success along the way.

However, treating our kids like they are a task to tackle or a project to persevere through will only hurt everyone in the long run. Our kids are not written objectives on a to-do list; they are human souls!

Let's begin instead to view parenting as a lifelong role we are called to fulfill. And more than that, it's a high and holy calling. It's the pouring into and shaping of future lives and generations.

## Four Life-Giving Choices of Love-Centered Parents

Now that we've talked about what is not our job as a parent, I want to discuss what our job is as a parent. I believe there are really only four jobs we have as love-centered parents. And I hate to even call them *jobs* because that sounds so stuffy and tiring. Instead, let's call them four life-giving choices we can make as a love-centered parent.

These choices have the potential to completely transform your parenting. And guess what? None is dependent upon your child's response, age, attitude, or decisions.

Throughout the rest of this book, we're going to be diving deep into each of these choices. I'm also going to give you specific practical ideas for how to walk these out in everyday life.

But for now, let's just briefly discuss each of these:

### *Choice #1: Lean In and Love*

When our kids are going through hard times, what they need most is for us to lean in and love them.

This requires a posture of humility and approachability. It communicates to our kids: I care about you. I'm here for you. I'm not going anywhere.

It doesn't matter what they have done. It doesn't matter what they have said. It doesn't matter if they have royally messed things up. We can still choose to lean in and love.

For our young kids, this could mean getting down on their level, holding them tight, looking into their eyes, sitting with them, snuggling close to them, and just being present with them.

As our kids get older, this might look more like stepping into their world, being interested in what they are interested in, inviting them to do something with us that they love to do, and/or embracing their God-given gifts and strengths—even if they are very different from our own. We can walk alongside them to help them pursue what they are passionate about and the unique way God has wired them, instead of trying to make them into someone we think they are supposed to be.

It's easy as parents to want to jump toward fixing a situation or coming to a quick resolution, but one of the most effective responses we can have is to shower our kids with the love of Christ.

We'll talk more about how to practically walk this out in chapter 5.

### Choice #2: Listen Well

I'm not naturally a good listener. On the contrary, I have the gift of words. (Some might not call it a gift . . . *ahem*!)

My tendency is to verbally process situations with my kids. I go straight into sermon mode, expecting them to listen while I talk through my feelings about their actions and behavior.

In the last few years, I've learned the value of waiting before I launch into a long lecture and to instead lean in and listen first.

For instance, recently we got an email about one of our children's behavior at school. It was uncharacteristic and a little surprising. Instead of meeting them at the door prepared with a speech on how they shouldn't engage in such actions, I waited until we had first reconnected after their day at school.

Then I said, "Hey, I got this email today. Can you tell me about it?" Allowing them to share their side of the story and what went down from their perspective was very insightful and opened the door for us to have a great conversation.

Had I started with a sermon or shown disapproval and frustration over their actions, this child likely would have shut down, gotten defensive, and felt completely unheard. Since I started the conversation with a question and a willingness to listen, they felt comfortable sharing.

Listening well also involves thinking before you speak, learning to hear what your child is trying to communicate (with their actions, attitudes, and behaviors), interacting instead of reacting, and becoming a student of your child.

We'll discuss this more in depth in chapter 6.

### Choice #3: Lead with Humility

So much more is caught than taught when it comes to parenting. Yes, our words matter, but the life we live in front of our kids is a much more powerful message.

Leading with humility involves setting a great example for our kids—on the good days and the hard days. It means being willing to ask for forgiveness when we've messed up, acknowledging our shortcomings and failures, and focusing on parenting our kids out of a heart to develop a relationship with them instead of trying to uphold our reputation with others.

Oftentimes, it will mean receiving truth from our kids that we might not want to hear (such as when they call us out for being hypocritical) or bringing in outside help in the form of counselors or therapists when our kids are struggling.

Ultimately, it's about living a life that shines Jesus before our kids. As Jeannie Cunnion posted on Instagram a few years ago, "We're not meant to be our child's savior. We're meant to point them to the Savior."[1]

Do our kids see an example of Christlikeness in us that they would want to emulate? Are we saying we love God and want to honor Him and yet we're going about our day with an attitude of frustration, anger, and unkindness?

We'll unpack this idea of how to lead with humility in chapter 7.

## Choice #4: Let Go

Not too long ago, I sat with one of my kids while they expressed how upset they were over some conflict and hurt they'd experienced in one of their friendships. As they shared their big feelings, I realized there wasn't anything I could do to fix their frustrations or alleviate their annoyance. All the words of comfort I tried to share and the encouragement I attempted to give fell flat.

More and more, as my kids have gotten older, I've felt God asking me to release them and let go of my desire to make sure that everything runs smoothly in their world.

In fact, even Jesus says that trials and struggles are going to be part of our world in John 16:33: "I have said these things to you, that in me you may have peace. In the world you will have tribulation. But take heart; I have overcome the world."

As we'll address later in the book, when I stop micromanaging my kids' lives, I give them opportunity to deepen their faith and trust in the Lord.

Yes, I still want to support them and provide guidance when they ask for it. I want to lean in and love. I want to listen well. I want to lead with humility. And I want to be a safe place for them to land when they need comfort and reassurance.

But ultimately, I have to let them go. They have to wrestle through their beliefs and convictions. They have to grow wings and fly. They need to process through hurts and hard things.

And it's okay if I don't have solutions or answers or quick fixes. Yes, it's hard for my mama heart; I want to swoop in and rescue and be the hero. But sometimes the greatest gift I can give my kids is to let go and sit on the sidelines cheering for them.

In this case, with my frustrated child, I sat and listened. And then I prayed. I asked God for wisdom. I asked God to help this child have wisdom and a calm, loving spirit as they walked through a rocky season in this friendship. I asked Him to help me know how to love well as a parent. And then I released my child to Him.

Nothing changed right away. My child was still agitated, and I still didn't have any good answers. But my heart was at peace—because I knew my child was (and is) in the hands of a God who sees the end from the beginning and loves them infinitely more than I can even imagine!

Letting go means not only allowing our kids space to grow up, to take more responsibility, and to have more freedom, it also means letting go of what we thought life might look like, what our hopes and dreams might have been for our family, and loving our kids even when they make big mistakes or have different viewpoints than we do.

Our kids are not going to be carbon copies of us. They are uniquely designed and uniquely gifted. They have passions and skills and interests that probably are very different from ours.

Letting them express their individual personalities, experiment with new ideas, pursue their passions, and (most likely) fail or experience discouragement in the process can be hard but oh so good. We can be right alongside them cheering them on, loving them, believing in them, and providing a safety net of love for them as they grow up.

Don't clip your kids' wings or try to make them into what you think they should be. Support them as they jump out and try flapping their brand-new wings, and watch them learn to soar in their own unique way.

We'll discuss this more in chapter 8—including the struggles and mistakes I've made along the way.

The beauty of these choices to lean in and love, to listen well, to lead with humility, and to let go are that they are not dependent upon our kids' choices, responses, or actions. Loving well doesn't require our child to obey, to be kind, or to love us back.

While I was writing this chapter, I got a message from a follower on Instagram asking me if I was nervous about writing a parenting book in light of the fact that I am starting over again with baby number four. She said something to the effect of, "Are you anxious that your fourth child is going to be a complete wild card?"

*Loving well doesn't require our child to obey, to be kind, or to love us back.*

One of the things I considered at length before writing this book was how it might impact my kids. I didn't want them to be burdened by feeling they needed to live up to a certain standard because their mom had written a book on parenting.

We had a lot of conversations about this as a family. In the end, we all agreed that it was the right thing for me to write it, and everyone gave their blessing. But I also realized that the heart and core message of this book isn't about your children's behavior; it's about how we love our kids as parents. This has been further solidified for me as I've written the book—and I hope it's what you end up taking away from reading it.

So, when I got that message on Instagram, I could truthfully respond that I'm not one bit anxious about what this child's personality will turn out to be because the point of the book isn't about raising great kids, but about leaning in to Jesus so we can love our kids well.

If we're being honest, we are all wild cards, aren't we? Our children, and we their parents. We are all wild and wonderful and weird and different and unique and special in our own way. There is no cookie-cutter parenting formula, because no child fits in a mold. Our love-centered Father in heaven loves every one of His wild cards, and He so beautifully displays for us that He desires relationship first and foremost, not results.

**"So you are no longer a slave, but a son, and if a son, then an heir through God" (Galatians 4:7).**

When we love our kids as our heavenly Father loves us, there is so much freedom! It's no longer about results-based parenting for a perfect kid but love-centered parenting that meets every child as a treasure to be loved.

In the chapters to follow, I'm going to flesh out what I have learned about these four life-giving choices. I can't wait to share with you how these truths have transformed my parenting.

But before we talk in-depth about that, I want you to know that I don't always live by these principles. Some days I still get frustrated. Some days I still say shaming, wounding words. Many days, I ask forgiveness.

But little by little, I'm becoming a gentler, calmer mom who cares much more about my relationship with my kids than I do about their making perfect decisions or about whether other people think I'm a good parent.

And while I've not been focused on results, it has changed our home in surprising ways. I'll share more about these in the coming chapters as well, but for now, here's a little peek from an Instagram post I shared in September 2017 because I want you to know that these principles really can change things, no matter how much you think you're failing as a parent:

> This year, as I've changed the way I've parented, my relationship with my oldest has grown so much richer.
>
> We used to butt heads a lot; now she's one of my closest friends.
>
> I used to struggle to get her to open up. Now she and I have long heart-to-heart conversations multiple times per week.
>
> She tells me often, "Mom, I love when you hang out with my friends. They all think you're so cool. And I do, too."
>
> I'm so grateful that God opened up my eyes to how I was micromanaging my kids and helped me to change from parenting for behavioral modification to parenting out of a heart to point my kids to Jesus and the Gospel.
>
> I'm a work in progress, but the fruit of these changes in my relationships with my kids has blown me away.
>
> Last year, I just didn't know how I was going to survive the teen years. Now, I can say with all honesty, I'm excited about them! Thank You, Jesus![2]

Change is possible. It's not too late. You're not too far behind. With a love-centered heavenly Father leading you, you can make changes that will impact the way you see yourself, and the way you see your kids. Freedom is coming. Let's do this.

## TWO TRANSFORMING TRUTHS
### for Love-Centered Parenting

1. I can't control the outcome or the results of my parenting. Only God can change someone's heart. My kids' choices,

behavior, morals, and character are ultimately not something I am fully in charge of.

2. Loving our kids well doesn't require our child to obey, to be kind, or to love us back.

# Lean In and Love

I thought I was a patient person . . . then I had kids.

I said I'd never yell at my kids . . . then I had kids.

I pictured myself as a sweet, loving, always-cheerful mom . . . then I had kids.

Motherhood has stretched me and humbled me. It's brought out the best in me and the worst in me.

Some of the worst things it has brought out in me are my anger, frustration, and irritability. For years I struggled to be loving and patient with my kids. I often found myself snapping at them and then feeling upset with myself that I wasn't more patient.

I felt trapped in this vicious cycle. The more I snapped at my kids, the more frustrated I was with myself. And the more frustrated I was with myself, the more I'd snap at my kids.

As God began to show me how much I was loved by Him, I started praying and asking Him to help me to love my children the same way He loves me, to have more patience, and to stop getting so angry with them.

As I was praying, an idea was birthed in my head. I decided to make a commitment that every time I was tempted to lash out at a child, I would instead find a practical way to love that child.

It was a big commitment, so I told my husband about it, and he agreed to keep me accountable. In addition, I began praying every day that God would help my kids to feel loved by me.

In the beginning, it was very, very difficult. Remember how much effort and commitment it took for me to replace lies with truth? Well, it required a similar process to choose to lean in and love instead of lash out.

It didn't happen in a day or a week, and it required prayer, the grace of God, and a plan. It wasn't enough to say, "I want to stop yelling and getting frustrated at my kids." I also needed to have something to do instead of lashing out. And so the mantra "lean in and love" was born.

When I was tempted to lash out at a child, I quietly reminded myself, *Lean in and love*, and then I looked for a way to walk that out. It might be calling the child over to come sit next to me, looking for a way to praise or affirm the child, or doing something with the child. It might be just getting down on their level, looking into their eyes, and saying, "I know you're struggling right now, but I want you to know that I love you and I'm not going anywhere."

I also wore a bracelet for a few months that had gemstones for each of my kids as a constant reminder of my desire to live a life of love toward my children, show love in tangible ways, think loving thoughts, and respond in love.

Every time I looked down at my wrist, it was there reminding me of my commitment to lean in and love instead of lashing out.

I've been listening to the book *Peaceful Parent, Happy Kids* while writing this chapter. It's been on my shelf for a long time, but

I recently discovered that the audiobook was available to download free from the library.

While I was getting ready for the day today, this sentence caused me to put down my mascara wand and quickly pick up my phone to email this quote to myself:

"You don't yell at a flower that isn't thriving; you water it."[1]

This quote was especially appropriate because I had a vase of flowers sitting on my kitchen table that were starting to droop in a sad way. I was worried they were a lost cause because they looked so pathetic. The very same day I heard that quote, I added more plant food and water, and within two hours, they looked like a completely new bunch of flowers. See? It even helps cut tulips!

How often do we get frustrated with our kids because they are struggling or seemingly not thriving instead of looking for ways to "water" them? What if, instead of expressing irritation or anger at our kids in these moments, we were to choose love, to look for ways to speak life, to smile, to step into their world, hold them close, and show them how much we love them?

One morning a few years ago, I was feeling really worn down as a mom. I had lost sight of how much I was loved by God and was trying to white-knuckle my way through a difficult parenting situation. One child in particular had been mouthing off and acting out, and nothing I said or did was making any difference.

I texted a friend: "Wondering if I'm just totally failing as a mom and wondering what on earth I am doing wrong, and what do I need to change??"

This friend texted back and reminded me that both Jesse and I are perfectly made to be this child's mom and dad. Then the friend encouraged me to let the love that God has given inside of me flow freely so that my child could see God's love through my actions.

It was such a simple encouragement to stop stressing over what I think I should do or shouldn't do, what I should or shouldn't change. To stop beating myself up and fixating on how I may have failed. To stop worrying about whether this child's heart is ever going to change.

Instead, to focus on the truth that God has perfectly equipped me with everything I need to be the parent of the children He has given me, and focus on loving my kids like Jesus loves them.

"Love them like Jesus loves them." That became another mantra for me, and it completely changed my attitude and approach in this situation.

> *God has perfectly equipped me with everything I need to be the parent of the children He has given me.*

In fact, I pulled this child aside and shared what God has been teaching me about how much He loves me. I asked them how they feel loved and how I can make them feel more loved.

We sat and talked and shared our hearts. They shared how they felt hurt and misunderstood in certain situations, and they felt as though no one understood. I was able to share examples in my life where I've felt the same way.

It was a beautiful moment and gave me a profound window into this child's heart and soul. And I would have missed this had I been fixated on just fixing the issue.

Jesus cares most about our hearts. He doesn't care that we have all our ducks in a row, that we do things perfectly, or that we get it all right. He loves us in our brokenness and mess-ups. He loves us even when we forget how much we are loved by Him and try to do things in our own strength.

He was the ultimate example of what it looks like to lean in and love. He left His perfect home in heaven to come down to this sinful world in order to show us His amazing love by dying for us on the cross. Not because we deserved it or earned it, but because He loves us. I want to lean in and love my kids as a reflection of the lavish love my heavenly Father has poured out on me.

**"In this the love of God was made manifest among us, that God sent his only Son into the world, so that we might live through him. In this is love, not that we have loved God but that he loved us and sent his Son to be the propitiation for our sins. Beloved, if God so loved us, we also ought to love one another" (1 John 4:9–11).**

Over the past few years, as I've shared this Lean In and Love concept with other parents, the question that always comes up is, "How do you actually do that? What does it look like practically to lean in and love?"

First off, the good news is that if you are a child of God, you have the Holy Spirit living in you. (See John 14.) You do not have to figure out life on your own and you do not have to live life in your own strength.

## Crying Out to the Spirit

You are filled with the Holy Spirit and you can call on Him for help and wisdom at any point in time. (See 1 Corinthians 3:16.) Do you realize what a gift this is? I think we often forget that we don't have to do this alone!

My first recommendation for how to practically lean in and love is to cry out to the Holy Spirit in those moments when you want to get frustrated, lash out, or yell at your kids. Ask the Spirit to give you calmness, strength, and the appropriate response.

I love the promise given to us in Jeremiah 33:2–3: "Thus says the LORD who made the earth, the LORD who formed it to establish it—the LORD is his name: Call to me and I will answer you, and will tell you great and hidden things that you have not known."

Ask Him to help you know how to show your child love and what that looks like right now for your child. I have found that He is so faithful to answer these prayers.

In case you were wondering, in these moments, I often can't stop and get on my knees and pray. I might be at the grocery store, or in the car, or in the middle of making dinner, so I'll send up a quick, nonverbal "flare prayer" such as, "Spirit, help me! I'm overwhelmed. I'm feeling anger rising inside of me. I need your help to know how to show this child love. Give me a creative idea and help them to feel your love flowing through me to them right now."

Or sometimes, I don't even have all those words and I'll literally just say, "Spirit, help me! Help me!" (See page 203 for more Flare Prayer ideas.)

Trust me, we don't need eloquent words or impressive prayers for God to hear and answer. In fact, Matthew 6:7–8 says, "And when you pray, do not heap up empty phrases as the Gentiles do, for they think that they will be heard for their many words. Do not be like them, for your Father knows what you need before you ask him."

A simple "Help me, Jesus!" or "Help me, Spirit!" cry for help acknowledges our need and our dependence upon God, and it can make a world of difference. He knows what we need, even when we don't know what to pray or how to ask for it. (See Romans 8:26–27.)

## 10 Practical Ways to Lean In and Love

In addition to crying out to God for help, here are some ideas that have worked well in our home as I've sought to lean in and love our kids.

### 1. Invite your child to be with you.

I've noticed that when my children are frustrated and acting out, it's often because they are craving attention and affection.

Inviting a child to come sit next to me or do something with me when they are getting on my last nerve can be so hard for me to do. In fact, I usually want them to be as far away as possible. But typically, distance is only going to make matters worse.

It can be our impulse to tell a child who is misbehaving, "Go to your room. You're in a time out!" But what if we flipped the script and instead gently said, "I love you so much and I want to spend some extra time with you right now because I've not gotten to be with you enough. Can you come sit with me?" Or maybe you invite them to work on a project with you, run an errand with you, help you with a task, read together, or watch something together. Whatever it is, make sure it is something that will be calming for both of you.

Lovingly asking my child to come sit next to me and be with me often helps to de-escalate the tension. It helps me to communicate love for the child (even if I don't feel all that loving at the time), reminds me that I want to prioritize love, and causes the child to feel special and cared for.

By the way, never underestimate the power of a loving touch. Whether that's snuggling with a young child, rubbing a preteen's back or shoulders, or putting your arm around your teen, your kids (and you!) need physical affection. If this wasn't modeled for you growing up or doesn't come naturally, it can be a challenge and it might feel awkward, but it is a very important way to express love to your kids through physical touch.

### 2. Stop, look, and listen.

We can get so busy with life. We have places to go, things to do, messes to clean up, meals to fix . . . the list is never ending.

Our kids don't need our productivity. They need our presence.

If a child is misbehaving, don't shush them just so you can get back to what you were doing. Stop, look into their eyes, and gently ask, "Is everything okay?" Or, "What's wrong?" Then really listen to their answer.

On a road trip a few years ago, when we had hours all together in our car, I asked our kids if they would answer the following two questions honestly: "How do I make you feel most loved?" and "What do I do that makes you feel most unloved?"

If I'm being honest, it was difficult to hear their answers (and even more of a challenge to receive them without trying to defend or explain myself), but I learned so much about my kids through these two simple questions.

Most of their answers revolved around T-I-M-E . . . how much they love and want to spend time with me. Both quality time and quantity time.

They said they want to know that their voice matters. That I care deeply about what they are interested in.

*Our kids don't need our productivity. They need our presence.*

In addition, they called me out on not always fully listening when they are talking. They want to know that I want to hear what they are excited about.

When they show me their artwork or creation or experiment or project, they want me to show genuine interest and enthusiasm and ask questions about it, praise specific parts of it, and appreciate the effort they put into it.

It's so easy to get busy with life, with our own projects, with keeping everyone fed and clothed and on track, that we fall into a rut of not really paying attention.

Sure, we might act like we are listening, but when they are talking a mile a minute, are we actually thinking about our own projects and to-do list while saying "uh-huh" and nodding along and responding "oh wow" or "cool" without really stopping to appreciate these amazing people and their gifts? I have been guilty of this so often!

Our kids are more perceptive than we realize. If we stop listening and paying attention when they are younger, they will eventually stop talking to us and find someone else to share their accomplishments and excitement and interests with.

I want to be my kids' biggest cheerleader. I want them to know that I've always got their back. That I'm always for them. And even if no one else cares, I will always care. The best way to begin to communicate this to your kids is to take the time and make the effort to really listen and pay attention to them.

As a result of my conversations with them on that road trip, I've been prioritizing listening, paying attention, noticing, and genuinely caring about what my kids care about. It requires effort, sacrifice, and time. But I truly believe it's one of the best investments I can make right now.

We'll be talking more in-depth about the power of listening well and learning to really communicate with your kids in the next chapter.

### 3. Be interested in what they are interested in.

"I'm at my wits' end! I can't seem to connect with my daughter at all! It's like she just doesn't want to have a relationship with me," a distraught mom confided to me recently.

My heart went out to her, and I asked some questions about the situation, including, "What does your daughter like?" and, "What is she interested in and passionate about?"

After the mom listed off things, I said, "What would it look like for you to step into her world and be interested in those things with her?"

The mom abruptly responded, "Oh! I couldn't do that! That's just not me!"

Here's the thing I've learned from doing it all wrong: We can't expect our kids to love all the same things we love and get excited about.

I used to get frustrated because my kids were so different from me. But then I began seeing that their wildly different interests were an opportunity for me to learn and grow and expand my world. My kids have taught me so much about subjects that I used to have zero clues about. They have helped me develop new interests and skills. They've stretched and pushed me outside my comfort zone.

For instance, Kaitlynn absolutely adores Bath & Body Works. I'm not much of a shopper. I don't spend a lot of money on purchases that aren't necessities. And the thought of hanging out at the mall and trying scent after scent isn't really my cup of tea.

However, because I love my daughter, I care about what she cares about. So I ask her about it. I take her shopping at Bath & Body Works on occasion. In turn, I've learned all about their scents and sales and money-back guarantee.

Recently, she and I went to shop their semi-annual sale with her well-researched list, her gift card, and a coupon. She floored me by getting two bags full of stuff for only $10.80—and saving $98!

As I watched her strategically shop, I thought, *I would have missed this had I not been willing to set aside my "I don't like to shop or go to the mall" mentality and jumped in and embraced something my daughter loves.*

Stop expecting your kids to step into your world and instead start showing up in theirs. Ask them to tell you the details of the project they are working on. Go sit with them while they are watching something and show interest in it. Let them try to teach you how to do things they are good at. (This can end up in lots of laughter and memory making!)

And please know this: It's okay if you don't ever care about what your child is passionate about as much as they do. You might not develop a new skill or interest in line with theirs. But you can still ask questions and show interest and be willing to learn because you love your child. When you love someone deeply, you also care about what they care about.

In addition, take time to invest in the people they care about. Ask them about their friends. Make your home a welcoming space for them to invite their friends to. When they have their friends over, be genuinely interested in their friends' lives too. When your kids see that you love and value some of the most important people in their lives, it goes a long way. It also helps you to understand the highly influential relationships in their lives.

> *Stop expecting your kids to step into your world and instead start showing up in theirs.*

### 4. Pray with your child.

When one of my kids is struggling, I'll often ask them if I can pray for them. They usually say yes. And by the end of my prayer, they are typically less agitated and in a much better mood. My willingness to take time to pray with them not only can help them feel loved, but it also communicates that we need God's help in our everyday life—especially when we're frustrated or overwhelmed.

A friend once shared another variation of this idea with me. She said when she's finding it difficult to respond with kindness and gentleness to her children, she'll ask them to gather around and pray for her. She said that it's basically impossible to respond in anger after your children have gathered around you and prayed for you!

### 5. Go outside and take a walk together.

If you feel like things are about to explode inside the walls of your house, call everyone together and tell them you're taking a walk in five minutes. (Or you can make it a family bike ride if you have older children.)

Exercise and fresh air can do wonders when people are uptight! Plus, a change of scenery can provide a better setting for talking through issues in a calmer manner.

Breathe in the fresh air, soak up the sunshine, and notice the beauty around you. This will boost your spirits for the tasks that lie ahead of you for the rest of the day.

If it's raining or there's another reason why a walk might not be feasible, try a change of scenery or plans—such as making hot cocoa and reading together or building a fort in the living room or going on a drive.

### 6. Share three things you're thankful for.

There is always something to be thankful for, but sometimes we can get so bogged down by all the problems, stresses, and struggles that we forget to count our blessings.

In those moments when you want to yell at your kids, challenge yourself to stop, take five minutes, and call your kids together, then each of you share three things you're thankful for.

This might seem difficult at first if everyone is at odds with everyone else, but force yourself to do this and it will most likely change the tone in your home. Plus, it might help you step back and gain some perspective: In light of all you have to be grateful for, the small things someone is doing that irritate you won't seem so upsetting.

### 7. Do something fun as a family.

If you have young children, this can be especially helpful to do on a hard day. When things feel like they are falling apart, set aside your to-do list and plans for the afternoon or evening and have a tea party, a family game night or movie night, or go do something fun together.

If your plans can't be set aside for the afternoon or evening, what about taking five minutes for a dance party, ten minutes to watch a few funny YouTube videos (we love to watch Tim Hawkins), or fifteen minutes for a game of Uno?

Sit down, smile, and enjoy your children. Take time to laugh together, read a story (or tell stories), and talk with them about how they are feeling about life or things they are struggling with, or even offer some encouragement for them in areas where they need improvement.

## 8. Put yourself in your child's shoes.

It's so easy for us to forget that our kids are often carrying heavy burdens too. Sometimes we can be so focused on our world and what we're carrying that we lose sight of what they might be sad or stressed about.

The other day, one of our kids was irritated at everyone. I realized something was bothering them, so I asked them to go have a few minutes of quiet. I reassured them that they were not in trouble but that I thought something was upsetting them and I wanted to give them time to think about what they might be feeling upset about so that we could talk about it.

I told them I would come back in five minutes and they could tell me what they were feeling. When I did, they poured out all sorts of frustrations while I just listened.

This simple exercise seemed to make a world of difference and allowed me to gain a better understanding of what this child was feeling and carrying.

We all need a little bit more grace! Some questions I've started asking my kids if they are not doing well or just seeming off or irritated are:

- What can I help you with? (Just knowing I'm there to help can make them feel calmer because they know they are not alone.)
- What are you feeling overwhelmed or stressed about right now? (This question helps them learn to stop and assess what they are feeling instead of letting their stress come out sideways as irritation or anger.)
- Are you scared, fearful, or worried about something? (Maybe they don't even realize they are afraid of

something. Stopping to ask might help them dig more into the root of their irritation.)

- How did you sleep last night? (Most people feel on edge or more emotional if they haven't had enough sleep. I know I certainly do. Maybe they need a quick power nap.)
- What did you eat today? (Pretty much all of us will feel tired, sluggish, and even frustrated if we are hungry. Make sure your kids have eaten enough.)

When kids are in a bad place or especially frustrated, however, asking these questions might only irritate them more. In that case, I review these in my own mind to see if I can identify any contributing factor that I could help relieve (such as making them a high-protein snack, sitting with them and calmly helping with a school project, listening well or making them laugh, suggesting they lie down and rest for fifteen or thirty minutes, etc.).

One of the most effective ways for me to show grace has been by putting myself in my kids' shoes and thinking about how I might feel if I were experiencing what they are experiencing, and about how I would want to be loved on and treated. I also think about how I can set a beautiful example of Jesus' love before my kids.

Not too long ago, one of my kids was disrespectful toward me. I told them that if this disrespect happened again, I would have to take away a certain big privilege.

Unfortunately, the next morning, they were disrespectful again. I quietly reminded them of what I had said the night before and told them they had lost the privilege.

They were devastated. And it broke my heart to have to take something away that was so near and dear to them.

It was also an opportunity for me to lean in close and let this child know how much I loved them and how sad I was that they wouldn't have that privilege.

The rest of that day, they had such a softened, changed heart, and we had a wonderful day together.

When I woke up the next morning, I felt the Holy Spirit prompting me to give that privilege back to the child. This is not usually how I would roll, but I couldn't shake this idea. I talked to Jesse, I thought about it, I prayed about it, and felt like it was the right thing to do.

A few hours into the day, I went back to the child and told them that I was going to give them back that privilege. They looked at me dumbfounded and said, "But I don't deserve it, Mom!"

"I know you don't," I quietly responded, "but I woke up this morning and felt like that's what God wanted me to do. I think He wants you to know how much He loves you."

My child was still overcome with shock, still reeling from how they didn't deserve this . . . and then they said to me, "That's *grace*."

My throat felt tight and my eyes welled with tears. *Grace*, which is by definition getting what we don't deserve. Sometimes we forget just how much grace God has heaped upon us. But in that moment, with my child, both of us got a very tangible reminder of just how much we are loved.

I share this not to say that you should not give consequences. Love-centered parenting is not about excusing bad behaviors or attitudes (we often have conversations and consequences for those) or raising kids who are codependent instead of independent, but about remembering to extend grace and to love well.

Before I jump to consequences, I try to stop and put myself in my child's shoes, and to ask the Lord to give me wisdom to handle each situation. Often, I've found that I want to say things like, "Go to your room!" or, "Everyone stop talking right now or there will be consequences!" And I do this because I want people to be quiet out of my own selfishness. I want a quick fix instead of wanting to take the time and effort to listen, lean in, and love.

*Love-centered parenting is not about excusing bad behaviors or attitudes . . . but about remembering to extend grace and to love well.*

Growing up can be hard, exhausting, and overwhelming some days. Sometimes a snack or a nap can resolve a whole lot more frustration and irritation than a lecture ever would. (Note: And sometimes I, too, need a snack and a nap!)

### 9. Play with your children.

When was the last time you played with your kids? I mean, really got down on the floor and engaged in their world or did something your older kids think is fun?

While I don't think we need to entertain our kids 24/7, I believe it's important to regularly take time to spend time with our kids doing things with them that they love to do.

I have learned so much about so many things, thanks to my kids. They've taught me the rules of hockey and baseball (thanks, Silas!), schooled me on all sorts of makeup, skincare, and fashion tips (thanks, Kaitlynn!), and introduced me to new music artists and shows I never would have heard of on my own (thanks, Kathrynne!). They've also taught me to lighten up and laugh more. We love to text or share funny memes, and the kids think it's hilarious when I try to use preteen/teen slang.

If you're having a bad day, here's an antidote: Think of what your children love to do (outdoor play, Legos, games, or dress-up,

107

hanging out, watching a movie, playing sports, playing video games, etc.), and tell them you want to hang out with them for thirty minutes or an hour (or however much time you have—even ten or fifteen minutes will go a long way) and do that with them.

Then just have fun together and give it your all for the allotted time. I bet you end up having as much fun as they will and, at least for a little while, you'll probably forget all about the bad day you were having.

Another option is to tell your child you want to spend thirty minutes or an hour—or however much time you have—doing something fun with them but that you need their help. You'd like them to pick what they want to do with you. (You might need to give them some boundaries if you have a child with expensive tastes who might pick going to the local theme park where tickets are $100 a pop!)

Most kids will love this, and it will make them feel so loved and valued. Plus, I'm guessing they won't soon forget their special date with Mom or Dad! (Note: If you have a child who is a planner or slower at making decisions, I recommend giving them a day's notice or maybe a three-hour heads-up so they have some time to think through options and make a decision!)

## 10. Take time to refuel your tank.

Making time to replenish your own supply is not selfish; it actually enables you to be a better parent, spouse, friend—and whatever other hats you wear.

If you're pouring into your family and never taking time to refresh yourself, you're going to feel burned out and exhausted. This inevitably will cause you to feel more irritable and frustrated.

What energizes you? What refills your tank? Carve out time in your schedule to make this a priority on a regular basis.

Get a baby-sitter, trade baby-sitting with another friend, ask your spouse to watch the kids on the weekend or one evening a week—whatever it takes to make time for replenishing your tank.

Making time for you—to breathe, to refuel, to feel energized again—will help you be a calmer, happier parent. And a calmer, happier parent is one who can lean in and love much better than a stressed-out and frazzled one.

- - - - - - - - -

I'll never forget the time, more than ten years ago, when one of the girls was working on a craft project. She was using scissors to cut some papers for her creation while sitting on the fairly new suede couch. (You can guess where this is going already.)

Unbeknownst to her, in her concentration to get the project cut out just right, she also cut the suede on the couch.

Not once, not twice, but five big cuts on the arm of the sofa.

She didn't even realize it until we were cleaning up the papers from the project. I saw the cuts first; then she did.

I wanted to get upset. After all, the couch was an expensive purchase and it was something we were intending to keep for many years.

But before I could become upset, a little voice whispered to me, *"It's just a couch."*

It wasn't worth anger or frustration—especially since it was an accident and she was immediately very sorry and upset about what she had done.

The accidental cuts she made on the couch could be mended with a needle and thread. Harsh words cutting into my daughter's heart couldn't be undone.

It's just a couch. It will fade, tear, and get stained with years and use anyway. It won't matter much twenty years from now. But my relationship with my daughter and how I respond to her—even in little things like this—will matter tremendously decades from now.

Instead of expressing frustration for her innocent mistake, we had a conversation about when and where to use scissors, and I told her we'd hand-stitch the couch and it would be totally okay.

We still have that couch and it still has those stitches in it. Every time I look at them, I'm reminded to lean in and love well.

## LEAN IN AND LOVE

When your new couch gets cut by the kindergartner, lean in and love.

When your quiet is interrupted and you feel annoyed, lean in and love.

When your child needs you over and over again, lean in and love.

When you feel frustration looming, lean in and love.

When your toddler asks you the same thing again and again, lean in and love.

When your three-year-old spills her juice and the dog knocks over the glass vase, lean in and love.

When that child is getting on your every last nerve, lean in and love.

When you are tired after a long day and your ten-year-old needs you to stay up and help with their homework, lean in and love.

When your teenager is struggling over something that feels petty, lean in and love.

When you feel irritation rising, lean in and love.

Lean in and love.

## TWO TRANSFORMING TRUTHS
### *for Love-Centered Parenting*

1. You are filled with the Holy Spirit and you can call on Him for help and wisdom at any time. You don't have to parent on your own!
2. Our kids don't need our productivity. They need our presence.

6

# Listen Well
# (aka How to Get Your Kids
# to Actually Talk to You)

Remember my struggling child whom I told you about at the beginning of the book? The one who was not allowed to continue attending the school they were enrolled in because of behavior issues, had to go to the ER because they were suicidal, was turned away by multiple counselors because the case was so complex, left us feeling completely at our wits' end as parents, and whom we had finally gotten in with a therapist who gently challenged me to consider how I could walk with my child in love instead of focusing on correcting them constantly?

Well, I thought it was time I caught you up on what transpired in the months that followed after hitting rock bottom in our parenting and the realization that I needed to completely change my approach to parenting.

Now, it's easy to say, "I had to completely change my approach to parenting." But what did that look like? It wasn't an easy process, believe me. In fact, it meant going back to square one and relearning how to parent. It was humbling, tiring, and a whole lot of work. But I'm here to tell you that it was worth every bit of effort.

It started with changing my core beliefs about myself. As I've shared in previous chapters, God used a number of circumstances and people to help shift the way I viewed myself and how much I was loved by Him. By His grace, I began to no longer see myself as not enough but as fully forgiven and loved.

This, in turn, changed the way I lived. Instead of living from the belief that I wasn't enough, I could live as loved. And I could live out of that love to everyone around me—including my kids. Little bit by little bit, instead of lashing out and responding in anger and frustration, more and more I found myself leaning in and loving my kids like Jesus.

It didn't stop with replacing lies with truth and living as loved, though. As we walked through that period of feeling utter despair and helplessness with our child, we spent so much time crying out to the Lord.

Jesse and I prayed together for God to give us clear direction, and I spent a lot of time crying in my closet, begging God for wisdom. Our prayers were often things like, "We don't know how to do this, God! This parenting thing is so overwhelming. Our child is struggling, and we can't figure out how to help them. Show us what to do!"

The answers didn't come all at once, or right away. But slowly, God kept showing us the next step to take. As I chronicled in chapter 2, the therapist encouraged me to focus more on walking with my child than on correcting them. The more I questioned why this had been my approach to parenting, the more I saw that

I had been going about things in such a detrimental way. I was trying to help my kids and instead I was hurting them.

## Rules-Based Parenting vs. Relationship-Based Parenting

Since the time my kids were little, I had prioritized teaching obedience as one of my biggest jobs as a parent. I had felt it was my role to raise my kids to always obey, instantly, and with a good attitude.

In fact, I repeated this to my kids often. I drilled it into their heads. "I expect cheerful, first-time obedience," I said more times than I could count.

When I look back, I see how I spent my days primarily focused on correcting my kids' wrong behavior, nipping their bad attitudes in the bud, and shutting down their complaining.

Those hours spent crying in the closet over my child who was falling apart at the seams broke something inside of me. I stopped wanting to parent according to my previous standards. I let go of my desire to try to produce cheerful, obedient kids. I simply wanted the opportunity to walk with my children and help them to know how much they were loved.

As I began praying for God to help me love my children wholeheartedly, I quietly felt the conviction of the Holy Spirit in my soul challenging me with this: "Instead of jumping to correct the bad behavior, first stop to listen to what your kids are trying to communicate through their acting out."

Wait, what? Whoa. I had never thought of it that way! It reminds me of Proverbs 15:1: **"A soft answer turns away wrath, but a harsh word stirs up anger."**

While I do want to lead, teach, and nurture my kids (we'll talk more about that in the next chapter), I had been so consumed with the goal of having kids who were well-behaved and obedient that I never stopped to listen to what my children were trying to communicate through their bad behavior.

*Instead of jumping to correct the bad behavior, first stop to listen to what your kids are trying to communicate through their acting out.*

Rather than focusing on building relationship, I was focusing on enforcing rules.

My heart hurts to say this, but as I started paying attention, little by little I recognized that my child who was struggling so much was feeling neglected and shut down by me. When I talked to them about this, they told me they felt like they could never make me happy or please me and that whatever they did was the wrong thing.

Their angry outbursts, their constant challenging of authority, their threats and tirades—at the root of it all was their trying to get my attention. They were crying out for affirmation, for acceptance, for quality time, for reassurances that they were a priority, and for me to show a genuine interest in their everyday life.

At first this was a hard pill to swallow, as I really thought I was already providing affirmation, quality time, and showing an interest in my kids' lives. And I struggled with feeling like I had totally ruined my child's life (and probably my other kids' lives too).

But I quickly realized that wallowing in feelings of failure and shame and guilt was not going to accomplish anything—and it definitely was not how God would have Loved Me live. So instead, I saw this as a fresh opportunity to learn from my mistakes and choose to change.

The more I stepped back and analyzed things, I realized that most of the one-on-one time I was spending with my kids—and especially with this child who was struggling so much—was actually devoted to correcting them, talking through issues, and giving mini sermons.

Let me say it again: I'm not discounting the importance of teaching and leading and communicating truth to your kids. I'm also not saying you should never correct bad behavior. But if you spend the bulk of your time telling your child no, pointing out what they've done wrong, and telling them how they need to improve, do you think they are going to feel loved, nurtured, cared for, and safe?

I'm going to guess they will probably feel like they can never measure up to your standard, aren't good enough, and are a disappointment to you. This was certainly the case with my child—and I later found out our other kids felt the same way. Also, there's a good chance they will transfer some of their beliefs about how you view them to how God views them.

In the weeks and months that followed that incredibly difficult parenting season, I began praying for God to change my heart toward my kids and to help me learn to listen and communicate well with them, instead of focusing on correcting their behavior.

I have been astounded by the difference this change of heart has made! As I gradually learned to parent from a place of love instead of legalist do's and don'ts, my kids slowly began opening up more with me, inviting me into the deep places of their hearts, sharing their feelings with me, and having fewer angry outbursts. More and more, they felt safe with me rather than shamed by me.

## Five Keys for Communicating Well with Your Kids

I want to share some of the most helpful principles I've learned when it comes to communicating from a place of love and practical examples of how I'm seeking to listen well to my kids.

### 1. Listen to the mundane details.

Parents of littles, please hear me on this: Pay attention to the mundane stories, thoughts, and details your little kids want to share with you. Really and truly listen to what they are saying— even if it's the fifteenth time today they have told you about the LEGO tower they are building.

It can be so easy to not fully listen to the everyday conversations, especially if you have a child who has a lot of words to share. However, if you are too busy to listen to your kids when they are younger, they will eventually quit trying to share things with you.

I talk to so many parents who are frustrated that their preteen or teenager won't talk to them. Preteens and teens don't magically start talking to you when they turn ten or thirteen or fifteen. It's something they develop through hours of your being willing to prioritize what they have to say when they are younger.

*If you are too busy to listen to your kids when they are younger, they will eventually quit trying to share things with you.*

Also, as my kids have gotten older, I've realized that some of the most important lessons they've learned have come from little conversations we've had in the midst of the mundane. And some of the best discussions I've had with my kids have happened in the everyday-ness of life. They were not when I took them out on a one-on-one date or when we'd planned something special.

Don't misunderstand what I'm saying: I think dates are fantastic, and it's something we try to do on a fairly regular basis. But usually the best heart-to-heart conversations happen during unplanned moments: when I'm driving them to a friend's house or activity, when one of the kids experiences a hurtful situation, after watching a movie together that had some confusing scenes in it, when a child has expressed anger or frustration about something, or when I've messed up and had to ask forgiveness from a child.

One thing I've found that opens up a free flow of conversation is to ask them for their thoughts or opinions on something. This might not work with a sixteen-year-old who isn't used to having these sorts of conversations, but if you begin such discussions when your kids are young, they will likely enjoy engaging in them with you.

My kids tell me often that they wish more adults respected their opinions and would listen to them and value what they have to say. We love to have in-depth conversations on all sorts of topics ranging from current events to theology to their thoughts on how to deal with a difficult situation.

Jesse or I will often bring up something we've been thinking about or a current hot issue in the news and open the door for conversation around it. We might say something like, "Here's what I've been thinking about . . ." And we'll proceed to share our thoughts, then ask, "What do you think?"

We welcome healthy debate and discussion, so long as people are kind and gracious. In fact, we want our kids to have their own viewpoints, beliefs, and convictions. We want them to grapple with issues, learn to analyze positions, and practice articulating their thoughts.

Relationships are about showing up consistently, in the good and bad, the monumental and the boring. Don't just show up for the deep conversations; show up for the long-winded explanations of their current project, the in-depth recap of a show they are watching or a book they are reading, and play-by-plays of what went down in their classroom or exactly what happened at recess.

If something is important enough to your child to share with you, it should be important enough for you to listen well. This communicates to them that you care about all aspects of their life, including their interests, their struggles, their worries, and their relationships, and that you are available to them.

Your investment of time and energy when they are little will likely pay off in big dividends as they grow older.

### 2. Be available when your child wants to talk.

We have both a night owl as well as an early riser at our house—and both children love to talk to me! I know this season will not last forever, and I am going to miss these late nights and early mornings with them. Someday, my kids are going to be grown and gone, the house will be quiet, and I'll get to go to bed and wake up whenever I want (well, unless a child calls me late at night or early in the morning to chat).

It's such a privilege that my kids want to share their hearts, tell me what they are thinking and feeling, and ask to hang out with me. And I want to prioritize time for it, even though it usually means rearranging my schedule or setting aside my to-do list for a bit or getting a little less sleep.

Two nights ago, I met a father who had just dropped his youngest child off at college. He looked me square in the eye and said, "Cherish every moment. Take advantage of every opportunity to be with your kids."

It might sound cliché, but it wasn't. And I want to take his words to heart.

With my working full-time, the extracurricular activities and ministry we're involved in, plus the kids' homework load, many days I only get to spend fifteen to thirty minutes one-on-one with each of the kids. But instead of lamenting that or wishing for a different life (because I know we are right where God has us), I'm learning to look for pockets of time each day to make myself available to them.

That might mean talking late at night or early in the morning, or inviting them to ride with me in the car when I run an errand. I try to give my all to them during those windows of time.

In addition, I try to be available as often as I can for the unplanned conversations. As you probably know, these conversations are not usually at a super-convenient time. But love-centered parenting isn't about doing what is convenient or easy; it's about showing up for our kids and loving them well—even when it requires a lot of sacrifice.

There are times when a child wants to have a really important conversation, and I truly can't because I have a commitment that can't be moved, but in most cases, we can make the conversation happen. And I try to do everything I can to prioritize those important conversations—even if it means moving a commitment or asking a friend if I can show up ten to fifteen minutes late for something.

I know some people will disagree with me on this, but I try to live my life in light of what will matter most twenty-five years from now. In almost every case, my relationship with my child is going to be at the top of that list!

Now, please know I don't always have an instantly cheerful and available spirit about these unplanned important conversations. In fact, one recent evening, there was a knock on our bedroom door. My first reaction was to feel annoyed. It was after bedtime, it had been a long day, and I was ready for the kids to be asleep.

I opened the door in a bit of a huff and almost said gruffly, "What are you doing?! Don't you know it's bedtime? Get in bed!"

But before those words could come out of my mouth, I stopped myself and looked into my child's eyes. And I saw sadness and hurt written all over their face.

"Can I come in?" they asked sheepishly.

All my annoyance melted away as my child shared their heart with Jesse and me while cuddled up on our bed.

About twenty minutes later, they headed back to their bed with a smile on their face.

I almost missed this beautiful conversation and opportunity for my husband and me to love on our child because I was more concerned about getting enough sleep.

Parenting is exhausting. As an introvert, it's easy for me to feel peopled out and want space. And I think it's important for us to take time to refuel and recharge, but not at the expense of our kids' hearts.

Here's what I'm reminding myself: Look into their eyes. Pay attention to what's really going on in their heart. And be willing to bend the bedtime rules a little sometimes in favor of communicating to a child how much they are loved.

We can't do everything, but we can do something. Let's stop focusing on trying to parent perfectly and instead focus on just showing up—even if it's a simple ten-minute conversation. Grab hold of those moments and opportunities, no matter what time of the day or night it is.

### 3. Let your child express the full spectrum of emotions.

Instead of trying to fix my kids or preach at them, I'm learning to practice the art of quiet listening.

I often ask my kids when they get into the car at school pickup or when they walk in the door at the end of the school day, "What was the best part of your day? What was the hardest part of your day?" And then I try to really listen to what they share and ask follow-up questions. (See the Conversation Starters on pages 207–208 in the appendix for more ideas on how to get your kids talking.)

If you don't usually ask questions like these, I must warn you that once kids know you welcome their honest thoughts, doing so can sometimes open the door to a trickle of frustration. Some days, it's not just a trickle—it's more like a torrent!

Their frustration and big emotions used to scare me. It was almost as if I asked how they were doing to assure my heart that all was well. But if they expressed feelings that seemed negative, I wanted to instantly shut those down.

In addition to wanting to shut them down, I'd jump to worst-case scenarios: What if the teacher senses my child isn't enjoying their class? What if my child can't hold their frustration in and it all boils out in an ugly way when others are around?

My fear was ultimately about what others would think and how my child and my parenting would be perceived.

This fear caused me to overreact if my kids weren't feeling happy and secure. I'd get uptight and stressed, preach a mini sermon about having a better attitude, and basically tell them sternly why they needed to get over their feelings and/or stop feeling irritated or upset.

Now, I didn't necessarily say, "Get over your feelings!" But that is, in essence, what I was communicating when I would freak out if they told me about something that angered, bothered, or just plain irritated them.

Guess what this accomplished? It shut down the communication lines with my kids and made them feel like they couldn't share their heart or feelings unless they were doing well.

Is this what we want as parents? Sure, we ultimately would love for our kids to always be confident, calm, and cheerful. But expecting that all of the time is a completely unreasonable standard. I certainly know that I am not calm, confident, and cheerful all the time, so it would be crazy for me to expect this from my child!

As God has been doing a work in my heart, helping me to stop parenting out of fear or for behavioral modification (we'll talk more about that in chapter 8), I'm learning to see the heart of my kids, to truly listen to them, to be okay with letting them air their frustrations and struggles without feeling like I have to go into fixer mode.

The unexpected result is that my kids often come to me first with their frustrations before sharing them with friends; I usually don't even have to ask! If they've had a bad day, if they are feeling irritated by someone else, if something feels unfair, if they feel they were slighted, or if they are just feeling overwhelmed, I'm usually the first one to know it. I see it as a privilege that they trust me enough to vent to me.

When they open up to me, I'm learning to listen, ask questions, empathize with them, pray with them, or just sit with them and let them know they are loved.

I've also come to recognize that feelings themselves are neither good nor bad. Feeling angry or sad or happy isn't right or wrong. It's how we choose to act on those feelings that is either healthy or unhealthy.

If we shut down our kids' feelings, they will only be able to stuff them down for so long. Eventually, those feelings will come out—and likely in a way that will do a lot more damage.

Also, I try not to immediately jump to giving solutions. Not everything needs to be tied up neatly with a bow or have perfect answers. You don't need to fix all of the problems. It's more important that kids feel you are a safe place to express their feelings and that you will listen to and love them.

If my kids do ask for counsel or input (or I feel it's a case where it's necessary to give it), I will offer it—but usually in the form of asking them more questions, processing with them, sharing what I would probably do in their situation, encouraging them to seek God and think about how He wants them to respond.

*You don't need to fix all of the problems. It's more important that kids feel you are a safe place to express their feelings and that you will listen to and love them.*

Ultimately, I want my kids to learn how to think through difficult situations in a healthy manner, how to respond in love, and how to seek God for wisdom on their own. If I always provide immediate answers or fixes for them, it doesn't help them learn these skills and instead keeps them dependent upon me.

And by the way, remember that your kids often express what they are feeling through actions and attitudes, not necessarily words. As Dr. Laura Markham says in *Peaceful Parent, Happy Kids*, "No matter how bad your child's behavior, it's a cry for help."[1]

Pay attention to what your child might be saying through their behavior. Are they needing extra love? Are they feeling left out? Are they tired or hungry or feeling insecure? They often don't know how to express their feelings in words, so they will use actions, attitudes, outbursts, or a thousand other ways to communicate them.

Instead of instantly snapping at them to "Calm down!" or to "Stop yelling!" or instead of saying something hurtful like, "That's it! I've had it with you! If you don't stop right now, you will be sorry," how about stopping and first thinking through whether there is an obvious reason for their behavior? Is there anything deeper they could be trying to communicate?

The more you model using words to communicate feelings and the more they watch you do it, the more natural it will become for them. But this takes time, effort, and practice.

The best way to help your kids learn to use words instead of behavior is to set an example by doing so yourself. Let them hear you say things like, "I feel sad today because of XYZ." Or, "I'm feeling really excited about this week because of _____." Encourage them to share what they are feeling too. We have a feelings chart that we keep on our fridge as a reminder of what the various feelings are and that they are all valid and important. (See the appendix for a feelings chart and how to access printable feelings charts you can download for free.)

One of our kids was frustrated about something on a recent Saturday morning. There was a lot going on, so instead of really listening to them or engaging them in conversation, I just said rather tersely, "You need to change your attitude right now!"

As soon as the words were out of my mouth, I felt conviction in my heart. Instead of taking a little time to lean in, love, and listen, I just told my child, in effect, "Get over it!" I know when I myself am frustrated over something, it's typically not just about that thing, but often goes much deeper. I want to remember this for my kids as well.

Maybe they are frustrated because they are sad or hurt or scared or overwhelmed—and it's coming out sideways as irritation or anger.

Think about it: If you're feeling frustrated or stressed, would you want someone to tell you to "Stop acting like that and change your attitude!"? I know that if someone said this to me while I was already feeling on edge, it would just make me feel more frustrated.

In addition, this communicates to the child, "Your feelings don't matter. So stuff them down and move on!"

When my kids express their irritability or stress, I don't want to shut them down. I want to see it as an opportunity to lean in and love, look for ways I can come alongside them, and ask how I can help. I want to sit with them and love them well through whatever they are feeling.

Yes, it requires more time and effort than saying, "Change your attitude!" But I think it's going to make a huge difference for them—and for our relationship—in the future.

Note: This can also apply to adults in our life. If you encounter someone who seems really irritated or frustrated, remember that there is probably something much deeper there and see it as an opportunity to lean in and love them well instead of just feeling frustrated or hurt by their frustration and irritability.

## 4. Become a student of your child.

One of the greatest gifts you can give your child, and one of the best ways to improve your communication with them, is to study them and learn how they are wired. No child is exactly the same.

Every child has his or her own personality and set of strengths, weaknesses, struggles, abilities, and interests.

It's so easy to fall into setting up grandiose expectations that our kids will fit into a mold we've created for them, or they will follow in the footsteps of an older sibling.

Sometimes these expectations come from wanting our kids to have or experience or be things we never got to have or experience or be as a child. Sometimes they come from just assuming they will like what their older siblings liked. Many times, if we dig down deep and ask hard questions of ourselves, we'll realize our motivation is to impress others. And other times, it comes from a hope for our child to be like us—to like what we like, to have similar interests, and to share in the things we love.

Your child is not a carbon copy of you or an older sibling or your friend's child. You aren't doing them any favor when you try to push them to live out your own never-realized childhood dreams or squeeze them into someone else's gifting or passions.

*Start paying attention to how God has uniquely wired your kids. Look for what makes them come alive.*

Start paying attention to how God has uniquely wired your kids. Look for what makes them come alive. Notice what they are most interested in, what they ask questions about and talk about most often.

Let them explore and chase after their own dreams and passions. As much as possible, provide them with supplies and space to pursue their interests. Be their biggest cheerleader.

Invest the time and effort into truly understanding how God has designed them at their core. Discover what gets them excited, what makes them scared, what they are passionate about, and what their pet peeves are. Find out what makes them feel loved, what causes them to feel most seen, and what makes them come alive as an individual.

The best way to learn more about how your child is wired is to spend time in their world, being available to them, caring about what they care about, and asking questions and listening intently to their answers.

Each of our three older kids is incredibly different, even though they all have certain traits that make them Paines.

For instance, Silas loves to go on dates with me, sit next to me and watch YouTube videos and political shows, and for me to show up to all of his games and watch intently. He's a math and history whiz, our sports fanatic, and the child who is very detail oriented and schedule driven; he needs to know ahead of time what the plan is and when we are leaving. (Since Jesse and I are both pretty laid-back and chill, Silas helps keep us in line! He's also the child who remembers pretty much everything and will often remind me of things I need to buy at the grocery store or of a phone call I need to make.)

Kaitlynn adores shopping with me, making things with me (she basically has never met a DIY tutorial she could not totally rock if she set her mind to it), watching hockey with me (and explaining the plays to me!), and giving and receiving gifts. Holidays and picking out the perfect gifts and receiving gifts that are very thoughtfully chosen are incredibly important to her. She's highly creative and always has a project or three going in various parts of the house. She loves caring for babies and animals, wants to be an exotic animal vet when she grows up, can memorize long passages with ease, and is very driven and self-motivated.

Kathrynne is one of the most compassionate and caring people I've ever met. We love to hang out together, watch shows, and often stay up late into the night talking and processing deep subjects. Her favorite things include spending time with friends (thanks to her, we are often hosting groups of teens—and I love it!), discussing politics, basketball and sports, difficult math problems (she finds them to be a fun challenge—clearly she did not inherit that trait from me), and taking care of babies and little children. She is also very intent on knowing what she believes and why she believes it.

Sometimes, I look at them and think, *How did three kids who seem so different from one another all get raised in the same home at the same time by the same parents?*

And yet, I love it so much! When I wrote much of this book, Kierstyn wasn't born yet, but Jesse and I couldn't wait to see how our sweet child would be different from the other three. She's only a baby, but we already see her unique personality emerging.

I love that I constantly learn so much from my kids. I love that they push me outside my comfort zones. I love that they expand my horizons, broaden my knowledge, and introduce me to concepts I would never consider or explore on my own.

It hasn't always been this way, though. Especially when it came to Kaitlynn. Like I said, she's creative. She finds joy and delight in experimenting, trying new things, DIY tutorials, and making things with her hands.

For the longest time, though, I didn't see much beauty in her creations. I only saw the messes she left in her wake (which to creative hearts aren't messes at all but spaces where beauty and life are birthed!).

I didn't appreciate the way God had uniquely gifted my daughter because I was so busy trying to stuff her into my neat and tidy box. All the while, I was inadvertently crushing her spirit.

Her soul needs to be creating. She can't not create. It's in her DNA.

I tried so hard to get this girl to be more like me and see things more from my perspective. I got frustrated that she was so different from me. I didn't understand that God had wired her that way and couldn't see that He knew I desperately needed more beauty and creativity and art in my life.

Slowly, I've come to realize that by celebrating and embracing who God has designed her to be, I learn so much. She's taught me that while God is a God of order, He's also a God who created beauty.

He could have made the world in black and white. He could have made just one kind of butterfly or one kind of flower—or none at all!

But He created a world that is bursting with color and variety—with no snowflake or sunset or fingerprint alike.

The heavens—and all their wonder—declare His glory. So our lives—as His image-bearers—can declare His beauty too.

The more I've stopped trying to squeeze her off-the-charts creativity into my organized little plan, the more I've discovered that she brings so much amazing-ness into my life. And the more I've fallen in love with this incredible girl and all her abilities!

I don't want to try to stuff her into a little box anymore. I want our home to be a canvas for her soul to breathe.

### 5. Get professional help when needed.

Some of you might be shocked to find out we've spent a lot of money on counseling/therapy for our kids in the last few years. Others of you might feel relieved.

That doesn't matter. I feel very strongly that sometimes bringing in professional help can be one of the greatest gifts you can give your kids. We've certainly seen how our whole family is better for it.

It has helped our relationships grow. It has helped us all learn to better express our feelings and emotions. It has taught me how to parent my kids in a way that helps them feel loved much more deeply. And it has removed the stigma that I once felt around paying for professional help.

Four years ago, when someone suggested counseling for one of our children, I felt condemned. But now, I will shout from the rooftops that counseling and therapy have been worth every penny.

Not only did it make a profound difference in my life and parenting, it has been the catalyst for incredible change in our home—especially when it came to our child who was struggling. The weekly visits with the therapist helped our child go from angry outbursts and inconsolable frustration to being able to communicate verbally that they were feeling sad or hurt or disappointed or scared. This allowed us to have a much better understanding of what our child was going through and how we could help them.

In addition, the therapist quickly determined that there were likely some mental health issues at play and was able to get us in with a doctor, who ran a bunch of tests, and we were able to get a formal diagnosis and medication that also have been a huge help.

Today, our child is a completely different kid. They still have the occasional struggle or setback, but they are happy, thriving, and healthy. It has been a journey and a process, but I am so thankful for how God has used wise professionals along the way, and I feel strongly that we would not be where we are today if it were not for them.

Note: I know the cost of therapy and counseling can often keep people from pursuing it. There are many low-cost and even no-cost options out there, if you're willing to look. I recommend checking with local churches and organizations to see what is available in your area. There are also online services that are often much less expensive. In addition, check with your insurance to see if it might be covered under your plan.

---------

When we were in the midst of feeling overwhelmed and pretty helpless in parenting our child who was spiraling out of control, I had the privilege of spending a few hours with Dr. Meg Meeker. Dr. Meg is a pediatrician who has spent almost thirty years writing, teaching, and speaking to help equip parents and children with the tools to live healthier, happier lives. She has written six books and has spoken to thousands of families; she is a wealth of wisdom.

It was such an honor and I was so humbled that she had reached out to me to see if we could get together when she was in town. As we sat at Starbucks drinking our cups of coffee and tea, I expressed to her my fears, worries, doubts, and feelings of inadequacy as a parent.

She looked into my eyes and said, "God has equipped you with everything you need to be the best parent to the children He has given you. Don't sweat the small stuff. Get the big stuff right. That's what matters."

Those words have stuck with me. God knew how much I needed to hear them. On days when I question whether I have what it takes, when I worry that I'm messing things up and making too many mistakes, when I wonder if I should have responded differently or asked a different question (or maybe pried harder or given more space), I go back to Dr. Meg's words.

Parents, God has equipped you too to be the best parent for the kids He has given you. You won't get all the small stuff right. You will make wrong choices. You will miss the mark some days. You will need to ask forgiveness. And you won't always respond perfectly or ask the right questions. The beautiful thing is that the hard stuff is meant to drive us to deeper dependence on God.

> *God has equipped you too to be the best parent for the kids He has given you.*

Best of all, God can use your inadequacies and your missteps in powerful ways in your kids' lives. We'll talk about that in the next chapter!

## TWO TRANSFORMING TRUTHS
### *for Love-Centered Parenting*

1. God has equipped you with everything you need to be the best parent to the children He has given you.
2. You don't need to fix all the problems. It's more important that kids feel you are a safe place to express their feelings and that you will listen to and love them.

# Lead with Humility

I opened up my email to find a message from a teacher saying that one of our kids had missed yet another assignment deadline.

This was the fourth email in the span of two weeks from a teacher to let us know that our child had turned in late work or missed an assignment. I began to get concerned, as this kid is usually on the ball.

I wondered if something deeper was going on. Was the child slacking off and getting lazy, or were they getting in with the wrong friend group? Were they upset about something or dealing with an issue they didn't want to talk about? Was it now showing up as poor performance at school?

After we received yet another email, I decided it was high time to have a conversation. Unfortunately, instead of praying and preparing for this conversation, I unleashed all my fears and questions on this child.

"Is something wrong? Is there something you aren't telling us? What is going on?" I interrogated.

My heart's desire was to help this child and uncover the root issue, but I was going about it incorrectly. After they said nothing was going on and they were just a little overwhelmed, I proceeded to launch into what I thought was an inspirational pep talk. I challenged them to aim higher, shared how I knew they were capable of doing well in these areas, and admonished them to develop more discipline.

I gave some suggestions and strategies and left the conversation feeling like I had given this child a much-needed kick in the pants. I thought I had handled the whole situation pretty well, since I hadn't shamed them or raised my voice.

But this child came away from the conversation with a very different perspective, I found out later. They felt I hadn't listened to them at all. They felt hurt and discouraged instead of fired up and motivated.

Thankfully, Jesse noticed that something was up when he was with the child later in the day and he asked about it. They ended up having a good conversation and this child opened up and freely shared their hurt and how they felt I hadn't listened to them.

When Jesse told me this, I felt so naïve and sad. I was trying to inspire my child and instead I ended up crushing their spirit and making them feel frustrated.

They didn't need a lecture from me; they needed the gentle, gracious listener Jesse had been. They needed to be encouraged, to have a place to vent their sense of being overwhelmed, and someone to offer to walk with them as they figured out how to better manage their time. I had sort of bulldozed them in the name of trying to motivate them.

When I realized how much my words had wounded my child, my heart felt so broken. I went back and asked forgiveness and was able to have an honest discussion about how I could have approached the situation differently. Though I couldn't repair all the damage I'd done, I could learn from this situation to do better at communicating my heart in the future.

This is what love-centered parenting is all about. It's not about always having the right responses or always making all the right choices all the time. It's about loving our kids, walking with them, and being honest and humble enough to admit our shortcomings and struggles.

Think about it. If we desire for our kids to admit when they make wrong choices or mistakes, shouldn't we lead by example? If we want our kids to be honest and humble, let's lead the way.

Leading with humility involves six key components.

## Acknowledge Your Need for Jesus

If we were perfect parents, we wouldn't need Jesus. The whole reason Jesus came to earth and died for us was because we aren't able to achieve perfection (Colossians 2:13–14). We will never do it all right—and that's not the goal. Our kids need parents who are honest enough to admit their mistakes and imperfections and their need for Jesus.

One of the greatest ways we can lead with humility is by not only acknowledging our struggles and shortcomings, but also expressing our need for Jesus in the midst of real life.

*If we were perfect parents, we wouldn't need Jesus.*

As Cindy Rollins writes in her book, *Mere Motherhood*, "Most mothers like to think there are perfect families out there. It makes them hopeful, but what should make them hopeful is that there are no perfect families yet. There is only redemption, offered to you and your family through Jesus Christ."[1]

Christ's finished work on the cross frees me up from having to live life chasing after pleasing other people, being a perfect parent, or managing my reputation. I don't simply want to teach my kids how to modify their behavior. I want to show them their need and my need for Jesus.

**"In him we have redemption through his blood, the forgiveness of our trespasses, according to the riches of his grace" (Ephesians 1:7).**

Every day we have opportunities to model how much we need Jesus, whether it's praying for His help in a difficult situation, acknowledging His protection when a car almost collides with us on the highway, talking with our children about how we are relying on Jesus through hard circumstances, or just taking the time to thank Him for answered prayer.

My heart in parenting is for my kids to see that my relationship with God is not a Sunday-morning thing but an hour-by-hour thing. Because I need Jesus each and every minute of each and every day.

There is no manual that tells me exactly how to parent and how to respond in every situation for each child. (Don't ya wish there were? It sure would make life a lot easier!)

But that's why I'm so grateful for Jesus. I can go to Him every day to ask for wisdom in my parenting, to beg Him to help me walk with my kids well, and to seek His direction for how to parent my kids in ways that they feel most loved. I can ask Him to give me clarity when I don't know the way and to plead with Him to fill in the parenting gaps I know are there, many that I don't see or recognize.

I'm learning that some of my greatest parenting happens on my knees, with open hands, entrusting my kids to their Creator.

## Ground Yourself in God's Word and in Prayer

We often think that a great parenting book, a fantastic chore chart, a really good schedule, choosing the right extracurricular activities, or spending a lot of quality time is going to make a big difference in our kids' lives. These things can (and do) make a difference. But more and more, I believe that the thing that will have the most impact on my kids' hearts and lives is their mama praying for them and pointing them to Jesus in the day-to-day of life.

Every morning I begin my day by walking on the treadmill, writing a few sentences in my gratitude journal, reading my Bible, reading a few chapters from some soul-filling books, and praying over my day. Part of praying over my day includes not only going through each activity and interaction that I know is planned for the day and asking God to help me be a light and to love well, but it also involves praying for Jesse and each of the kids.

Oftentimes, I'll pray specifically for something a child is walking through, struggling with, or feeling frustrated over. Maybe they have a test at school they are anxious about, or a situation with a friend they are navigating, or a big project they are tackling, or some health issues they are facing, or maybe they are just feeling frustrated and hormonal. I bring these issues to the Lord and ask Him for wisdom for my child and wisdom for me to know how to best walk alongside them through it.

Many times, later in the day, one of my kids will come and share with me something that relates to exactly what I prayed for them in the morning. It's always so fun to be able to tell them,

"I prayed this morning that that exact thing would happen!" I want them to know that God cares about them, that I care about them, and that God is in the business of answering prayers on their behalf.

Note: Your morning probably looks very different from mine, and you might not have uninterrupted or concentrated time to pray. That's okay! You can pray as you shower, as you get ready, as you pack lunches or make breakfast, or even as you drive. See more ideas for busy seasons on the pages ahead.

Leading with humility and pointing our kids to Christ also involves modeling what a relationship with Jesus looks like. Our daily choices show where our priorities really are.

If we tell our kids we want them to put Jesus first in their lives and yet they never see us taking time to invest in and pursue a relationship with Jesus, what kind of example does this set for them? As with any relationship, it doesn't just happen; it has to be intentionally invested in.

You might be thinking, *I don't have time to read my Bible or pray right now! I'm just so busy!* Well, if you have time to read these words, you have time to read God's Word. If you have time to scroll social media, you have time to pray. If you have time to stay up-to-date on your favorite shows, you have time to listen to worship music.

*You can't pour out Jesus' love to your kids if you never spend time refueling yourself with the truths of His love for you.*

As I've heard it said before, if it's important to you, you'll make the time. If it's not important, you'll find an excuse.

You can't pour out Jesus' love to your kids if you never spend time refueling yourself with the truths of His love for you.

If you struggle to make your relationship with the Lord a priority, here are a few practical ideas that have worked for me over the years.

- Get a copy of *Daily Light* by Samuel Bagster and read the morning and evening reading either first thing in the morning or right before you go to bed. (This is a compilation of Scripture on various topics—one page of verses for each morning and one for each evening. It comes in a variety of Bible translations, so pick whichever one you love best.)
- Hang Scripture around your house: on the fridge, above the sink, in your bathrooms, as a screensaver, on the mirrors—anywhere you'll see it regularly. (Note: See the Memory Verse cards on pages 215–219 in the appendix for some of my favorite Scriptures included in this book and a link to free downloadable Scripture cards you can print and cut out to post around your home.)
- Sign up for the Bible reading plans through SheReadsTruth.com or HeReadsTruth.com. I love that they have plans you can do with your spouse, if you are married. For each day there are a few passages of Scripture to read plus a short devotional. Occasionally, they release plans you can do with your kids too.
- Find a Bible reading plan on the YouVersion app or Bible-Gateway.com (or keep it simple and read one chapter from Psalms or Proverbs per day) to read aloud at the breakfast or dinner table to your kids each day. I've found it's so much easier to read aloud to my kids when they have food in front of them. Everyone stays a lot quieter!

- Ask a friend to keep you accountable for spending time reading God's Word every day. Maybe you could even text your friend something meaningful or a Scripture from what you read.
- Download the First5 app and commit to reading God's Word for the first five minutes you are on your phone each morning before you check your email, the news, or social media.
- Turn on worship music or the Bible on audio while you cook, clean, drive to work, work out, or fold laundry.
- Keep a list of prayer needs on your bathroom mirror to remind yourself to pray while you're brushing your teeth, washing your hands, shaving, or putting on makeup.

These are just a few ideas. There are so many others, and if you begin to look for creative ways to incorporate prayer, God's Word, and uplifting worship music into your day, I can pretty much guarantee that you'll find time to make it a daily practice.

## Set a Good Example

Notice this doesn't say "Set a perfect example." That's because we will never be able to attain perfection. (We'll talk about this more in a minute.)

But a good example is imperative. Leading well means that we aren't asking things of our kids that we aren't doing ourselves.

This is easier said than done. Oh, how I know that!

Recently, one of my children was yelling when I had asked them to stop. (They were horsing around and just being super loud. I'm sure that never happens at your house.)

What did I do? Oh, I loudly and insistently hollered from across the house at them to "PLEASE. STOP. YELLING!"

Um, way to go, Crystal. Great parenting example there. (I'm still working on leaning in and loving, so don't for one second get the idea that I have this love-centered parenting thing all tied up with a neat and perfect bow. My kids will be happy to testify otherwise.)

Parenting definitely shines a light on areas where we fall short. It also shows us how our kids can smell hypocrisy from a mile away.

Stop and ask yourself, "Am I expecting something of my kids that I'm not expecting of myself? What kind of example does this set before them?"

For instance:

- Are you asking them to keep their rooms clean when your room is a mess?
- Are you encouraging them to have a good attitude about tough situations and then you are constantly complaining and frustrated about your life?
- Do you tell them not to talk unkindly about others and then you proceed to repeat a story at the dinner table that puts someone else down?

I know, I know. I just stepped on my own toes by writing that. I'm still very much a work in progress, and my kids call me out on it regularly, which I appreciate because it keeps me humble and gives me yet more opportunities to acknowledge how much I need Jesus!

Our kids are watching us and paying attention to our actions. Our words are important, but the life we live before them is so much more important.

## Welcome Honest Feedback

In the desire to lead with humility, I want to be open to constructive feedback. I want my kids to feel the freedom to come to me and say, "Mom, when you did that, it seemed like you weren't having a compassionate spirit." Or, "Mom, yesterday it really bothered me when you responded to me like you did. I felt like you weren't hearing me and were just shutting me down."

Of all the people in the world, our kids know our shortcomings best and see our blind spots most clearly. Welcoming feedback from our kids can feel a little scary, but it has been the gateway to some of the best conversations we've had. It has opened my eyes to many areas in my life where I didn't realize I was not practicing what I was preaching, and has allowed my kids to trust me more and to be more open with me.

> *Our kids know our shortcomings best and see our blind spots most clearly.*

If you don't currently have this type of relationship with your kids, can I encourage you to get brave and begin taking steps to make it happen? This might mean sitting your kids down and telling them that you want to set a better example for them or that you are working on yelling less and loving more, but that you need their help.

Let them know you would appreciate them kindly and calmly reminding you when you start to seem upset or frustrated. It could be a simple phrase you ask them to say, such as, "Kindness, Mom," or, "Lean in and love," or something similar. Or maybe you can come up with a special signal your kids can give to alert you that you are beginning to get frustrated.

Asking them to provide accountability and help for you in this not only lets them know that you are a work in progress, but it also will give you crazy amounts of motivation to follow through with what you are committing to! And it opens the door for your kids to someday come to you and ask you to help them when they are struggling in an area.

## Acknowledge Your Mistakes

A few years ago, I told one of the kids, who was struggling with some relationships, that they could come and tell me anything. And I emphasized the word *anything*.

I had expressed to them how I didn't want them talking to others about this situation and their frustration, but that they could come to me and tell me everything they were feeling—no matter how ugly.

Soon after we had this conversation, this child got home from an event and began unloading a whole litany of irritations about a specific person to me. They were upset. They were irritated. And they poured out their feelings with passionate emotion.

Instead of just patiently listening, I flipped out inside and I only let them talk for a few minutes before I couldn't hold my own feelings in anymore.

"What's changed with you? Why are you all of a sudden having such an unkind attitude toward this person? This is not the child I've always known you to be," I blurted out without thinking.

This child looked at me with surprise and said, "I thought you said I could tell you anything. I thought you said it was okay to air my frustrations to you. I've felt like this for a long time. I just was scared to tell you because I was afraid you'd be upset."

Big OUCH!

I sat there stunned at what they said, immediately recognizing that I had totally missed the mark in this conversation. Instead of being a safe place, I'd been a judgmental space. Instead of fully listening, I quickly jumped to conclusions. Instead of processing with them and praying with them, I'd shut them down.

What was the root of all this? Sadly, it was more about *me.*

Rather than listening to my child's heart and hurts, I instantly began thinking of protecting my own reputation with others. I was worried about what other people would think. I was parenting for others' approval and thinking about where this situation might lead if my child's attitude didn't change.

And so, after my child called me out, I stopped right there and looked into my child's eyes, thanked them for shining a light on my hypocrisy, and acknowledged to them that it was wrong. What followed was a beautiful conversation about grace, responding like Jesus, and how it's just plain hard to love people sometimes.

Our kids see that we are fallible, have struggles, and make mistakes. I cannot stress how much of an impact it can make in our kids' lives if we are willing to own up to our mistakes. In fact, I feel one of the greatest life lessons we can send our kids out into the world with is an understanding that it's okay to fall down and it's normal to experience setbacks, and that none of us has cracked the code on perfection.

As I have found over the years, failure can be one of our greatest teachers. I'm a pretty hardheaded person and can be as stubborn as they come, which is why it seems that I often learn lessons the hard way. I make big mistakes, and sometimes I feel frustrated that I have to fall so hard in order to learn important life lessons.

But as my kids have gotten older, I've realized that so many of the mistakes I've made have paved the way for me to have really honest conversations with them and empathy for them when they are struggling.

For instance, not too long ago, one child failed to follow through and do something they were asked to do. As a result, they lost the privilege of getting to do something they were really looking forward to.

This child was very angry. And honestly? I wanted to be all, "I told you if you didn't do X, you wouldn't get Y. It's your own stinkin' fault." And that would just anger and shame my child.

But I stopped and resolved to lean in, listen, and love.

So I sat with them while they cried about losing this privilege. I told them gently that I knew it was hard for them and that I was sad too. I asked what was the hardest thing about it and let them express their frustration.

Once they stopped crying, I shared with them quietly about why we had made the decision we did. I told them how much we loved them and how much we wanted to spare them pain in the future by teaching them now that following through and doing the right thing is so important.

I then asked, "Do you want me to tell you about a time when I didn't do the right thing and the consequences that came from that?"

They sat up and excitedly said, "Yes!"

We sat together while I told them about the time I made a very bad choice and experienced six months of hard consequences as a result of that one choice.

When I finished my story, this child had a look of deep understanding on their face. I could tell that they felt seen, heard, and loved because I had shared my own story.

Our mistakes can serve as springboards for great conversations and relationship with our kids—if we are willing to be open and acknowledge them instead of pretending we have it all together.

*Our mistakes can serve as springboards for great conversations and relationship with our kids—if we are willing to be open and acknowledge them.*

## Ask Forgiveness Often

When I was seventeen and a brand-new driver, I accidentally crashed our family's van into the front of the garage attached to our house. I permanently ruined some of the brick, and my dad had to exercise quite a bit of creativity to patch up the area with extra trim and a planter to cover up the damage.

I was upset at myself for months over that accident. I replayed it over and over in my head again—wishing I wouldn't have been careless, wishing my reflexes would have kicked in faster, wishing I just wouldn't have been driving at all that day.

It was very embarrassing—especially since I felt I was old enough that I shouldn't have made such a "dumb mistake." But when Silas accidentally broke our front window while practicing his baseball pitching skills, I was grateful for that experience. It gave me the ability to be more compassionate with my son and to remember the shame I felt when I was a teenager.

Do you know what I remember most as an adult about the unfortunate van incident? Much more than the feeling of shame, I remember that my dad asked me to forgive him for how he responded to me when he first found out about the accident.

I don't recall the specifics of my dad's angry words when he learned I had smashed the van into the front of the garage, but I do remember him coming back the next day to apologize. That's what stuck with me from that day. Not my dad getting upset with me, but the fact that he was willing to acknowledge what he had done wrong and seek to make it right.

Here are three important lessons I've learned when it comes to asking forgiveness when you've wronged someone—whether it's your kids or another person:

- **Go first.** In many cases, there might be mutual hurt. Don't wait for your child to acknowledge what they've done wrong. Take the first step toward reconciliation.
- **Beware of blame-shifting.** When you are going to someone and taking responsibility for your mistakes, it can be easy to fall into blame-shifting or excuse-giving. Focus solely on what you need to own in a situation and don't point fingers at others or give excuses as to why you did something. (For instance, don't say, "I'm sorry I did that, but you were acting irrational.")
- **Actually ask forgiveness.** This might seem obvious, but I can't tell you how many times I've been tempted to kind of skirt around actually asking for forgiveness. Don't stop short or give a sort of vague apology, i.e., "If I've offended you, please forgive me." No, actually have the humility to say, "I was wrong when I did XYZ. Will you please forgive me?"

This parenting thing is a constant learning and growing experience. I make a lot of mistakes. I have to ask forgiveness often. I wonder what I'm doing that my kids are someday going to need counseling to process through.

But I'm so grateful that I don't need to be a perfect mom. I serve a perfect God who is able to fill in all my gaps and loves my kids even more than I do. And even when I make mistakes, I am still loved by Him.

He doesn't expect perfection; He desires faithfulness and a willingness to acknowledge my need for Him—hour by hour.

Our kids are watching and paying attention. I was reminded of this so vividly when I experienced a scary feeling one night in the middle of my recent pregnancy. It was around 10 p.m., and all of a sudden, my heart felt like it was racing and I just couldn't calm down.

As I lay in bed getting a little worried over how I was feeling and a little panicky that something was really wrong, one of my kids came and lay down next to me, put their arm around me, and said, "Mom, it's going to be okay. I want you to just lie here and breathe deeply. Don't talk. Don't stress over how you're feeling. Just breathe."

They stayed with me until my body calmed down, and I felt more relaxed. It was beautiful because my child became a tangible picture to me of how much I am loved and carried by my heavenly Father.

As parents, leading with humility means we give and give—especially when our babes are little and they need our constant care. Often it can seem like exhausting, thankless work.

We spend our lives doing the same thing over and over again. We wash and fold the same clothes. We do the same dishes. We change who knows how many diapers.

We make meals only to have our family be hungry almost right after they are finished eating. We wake up for middle-of-the-night feedings. We bathe little bodies over and over—only for them to go play in the mud yet again the next day.

We answer the same questions again and again. We give the same reminders countless times. It can feel monotonous and we might wonder if it's really making any difference.

I'm here to tell you that it's not pointless work; it's investing in the lives and souls of humans. It's nurturing and loving. It's holy work—even the mundane stuff. It matters.

We get to model Jesus' love in action to our kids. We get to set an example of a servant's heart. We get to be the hands and feet of Jesus to these little ones. We get to point our kids to Jesus and pour into them in their most formative years. And we get to acknowledge our struggles, admit when we are wrong, and experience their forgiveness.

Ultimately, we have the opportunity to show our kids what humble leadership looks like, and that's powerful stuff! And sometimes we get opportunities to see all that work pay off in big dividends as our kids model Jesus' love right back to us!

If you're feeling the work you are doing is mundane and thankless, picture me leaning in and looking into your eyes right now and saying this: Don't give up. Press on. Keep loving the people around you wholeheartedly. Keep investing. Keep showing up and leading with humility. It *is* making a difference—even if you can't see it right now.

## TWO TRANSFORMING TRUTHS
### *for Love-Centered Parenting*

1. Some of my greatest parenting happens on my knees, with open hands, entrusting my kids to their Creator.
2. I can't pour out Jesus' love to my kids if I never spend time refueling myself with the truths of His love for me.

# 8

# Let Go
# (aka Raising Adults, Not Kids)

As I am writing this chapter, our country and our world are smack-dab in the middle of one of the worst crises we've faced in years—the coronavirus pandemic (COVID-19).

Schools, churches, and most all nonessential businesses are currently shut down in order to try to slow the spread of the virus. Our city just set up a Safer at Home mandate that strongly encourages everyone to stay home unless you work in an essential job (such as healthcare) or are going out on essential errands (such as to get food or medical items). In addition, we are being encouraged to wash our hands religiously, stay six feet away from everyone (it's called "practicing social distancing"), and wear masks when we do need to go out of the house on an essential errand.

As a result, we spent a number of weeks almost 100 percent at home, not leaving for anything but basic necessities (and trying to make do without if we can) or essential medical appointments. (I'm thirty-six weeks pregnant while writing this, and we are fostering a medically fragile newborn who was born

153

prematurely, so some doctor's appointments are essential for us right now.)

We are not having anyone over, and every single thing that makes up our normal outside-the-home activities and life has been cancelled. Our kids' schools were initially closed for two weeks, but then they closed them for the rest of the school year. This is par for the course for most schools around the country. It goes without saying that none of us has ever experienced anything like this before!

This global pandemic is hitting every person in some way—whether through sacrifices they are making, financial struggles, working longer hours, job loss, having to cancel or postpone important events, worrying about the health of an immunocompromised loved one, or losing a loved one. No one is exempt from the effects of this deadly and contagious virus.

As a result, there is a lot of upheaval, many unknowns, and great unrest in our world. There is fear and angst, and pretty much everyone everywhere is being impacted in significant ways.

Originally, I planned that this chapter was going to be on letting go as parents. I had my outline mapped out and a lot of thoughts jotted down about what I wanted to share. But I had no idea that I was going to get a real-life, hands-on opportunity to truly let go as a parent.

It all started when our oldest daughter, Kathrynne, who was fifteen at the time, was supposed to leave for an international school trip. This trip had been planned for months. It was part of her school's annual Week Without Walls event—when all of the students go offsite to do hands-on learning, participate in volunteer and ministry projects, and take educational trips.

After looking at all of the options for Week Without Walls, Kathrynne chose to go with a group of girls on a nine-day trip to Suriname in South America. This had been planned, booked, and paid for months in advance. In the few months leading up to the trip, however, there were suddenly international rumblings of the new and deadly coronavirus. It was mostly isolated in China, but it looked like it might eventually make its way to the United States and other countries.

A few weeks before Kathrynne was supposed to leave, the virus began to spread rapidly outside of China. We started paying more attention to the details of it, watching the news vigilantly, and praying for wisdom about Kathrynne going.

Jesse and I were already a little apprehensive about letting her go on the trip in the first place. We fully trusted her, and she is an experienced international traveler, but still, it's hard letting your child go without you to be in a different country for nine days.

After doing extensive research, praying, getting wise counsel, and talking to Kathrynne, we felt it was still safe for her to go—especially since there were zero cases of the virus in Suriname, and it wasn't spreading very quickly in the U.S. yet. We sent her off with strict instructions to wash her hands constantly (she's a clean freak when it comes to germs, so we knew this wouldn't be a problem), a whole lot of hand sanitizer, and many prayers.

It was hard to say good-bye. Little did we dream that her trip was going to take a huge turn in a very different direction than we envisioned.

I'll tell you more about that in a bit, but first we need to have an honest conversation about letting go. I know, I know, it's not exactly a fun, lighthearted topic to discuss. There can be a mixture of tears and bittersweet feelings involved. And that's okay. But that doesn't change the importance of giving our kids the gift of slowly trusting them more and more and letting them go.

## Parenting from Faith Instead of Fear

As I've confessed in earlier chapters, I have a tendency to want to overprotect, bubble wrap, and micromanage my kids. I don't want them to get hurt. I don't want them to experience pain. And I want to keep them safe.

But this only makes them stifled, weak, and miserable. It doesn't allow them to grow wings or develop the backbone and courage to head into adulthood. Instead, it teaches them to be overly dependent on me instead of allowing them to be dependent on God.

Ultimately, this is parenting from fear rather than faith. It's doubting God and my kids, and stressing, worrying, and trying to control my kids and the outcomes of their lives.

What does it mean to let go as a parent? Letting go doesn't mean we just throw up our hands and throw caution to the wind. Nor does it mean that we don't care deeply about our kids, aren't intensely invested in them, or abdicate our responsibilities as parents.

*If we want our kids to grow in confidence in the Lord, let's start by modeling that in front of them and parent out of faith, not fear.*

I've learned a lot about letting go in the last few years—and I won't pretend that it's been an easy process. It involves courage, risk, and a willingness to let your kids make mistakes.

This can be tough because none of us want our kids to fail, experience disappointments, get hurt, or struggle. And yet, as I've learned in my own life, failure, disappointments, hurt, and struggles have been some of my biggest teachers. God has used these things to mature me, stretch me, and ultimately increase my dependence upon Him.

Isn't that what we want for our kids? We don't want them to live life in the safe zone, stifled by their fears or smothered by our worries. We want them to jump out, try new things, experience adventures, grow in their faith, and have a strong confidence and trust in the Lord.

If we want our kids to grow in confidence in the Lord, let's start by modeling that in front of them and parent out of faith, not fear. We can set an example of Joshua 1:9 before them: **"Have I not commanded you? Be strong and courageous. Do not be frightened, and do not be dismayed, for the Lord your God is with you wherever you go."**

I've learned that in order for my kids to develop stronger character, deeper faith, and reliance on God, I need to give them some space and be willing to

- stand on the sidelines cheering for them rather than trying to jump in and referee the game;
- provide a safe landing place for them as they practice flapping their wings even though they sometimes take a nosedive;
- watch them bravely step into new situations and sometimes make mistakes rather than paving the way for them to be 100 percent successful;
- remind them of the truth of who they are in Christ as they work on learning to use their voice and have hard conversations;
- ask questions to help them process rather than telling them the answers or what they should think;
- encourage them to grapple with their faith and convictions, not shy away from difficult questions, and come to their own viewpoints;

- celebrate and praise them for progress and tiny wins instead of constantly reminding them of where I feel they are falling short;

- listen much more and preach a lot fewer mini sermons;

- embrace them for who they are instead of trying to fit them into a box or mold of who I thought they would be;

- gently nudge them to step outside their comfort zone instead of allowing them to just play it safe and sit on the sidelines.

This can be such a difficult thing as a parent because there are no hard-and-fast rules for how to do this perfectly or knowing what the steps are to accomplish this. It requires diligently seeking the Lord, asking the Holy Spirit for guidance, and trusting God to give you wisdom for each tiny step. (Note: In the appendix, I have formatted the bulleted actions as a promise to your child. See Pledge to My Maturing Child on page 209.)

I told you that Kathrynne wanted to go on a nine-day trip to Suriname. But what I didn't tell you was that the simple fact that she asked if she could go was a *huge* deal.

Just five years before she signed up for the Suriname trip, she was scared and completely uncomfortable being around kids her age. She struggled regularly with panic attacks and anxiety. It started when she was around seven years old and got worse over the next few years.

She has always had such a beautiful heart to serve and to pour into others, so to see her being so anxious and clamming up almost any time she was with kids her age just about did me in.

We had many long talks over her social anxiety and how she felt lonely and left out. We tried putting her in different social situations to give her opportunities to grow, learn to reach out, and build genuine relationships. But each time, it ended in tears, stress, and fear over having to face kids her age again.

By the time she was eleven, she was at the point where she was avoiding kids her age as much as she could. We saw her closing up more and more and felt at a loss to know how to help her break out of her fear and anxiety.

We prayed. We encouraged her with new ideas. We kept trying new approaches. Nothing worked.

One day, as I was crying out to God for wisdom, I felt this strong prompting that the best course of action would be to put her in school instead of homeschooling. It seemed like a crazy idea, as I always assumed we would homeschool through high school graduation. I loved homeschooling and, in all honesty, there was some unhealthy identity and pride in my title as "homeschool mom."

I told Jesse this bizarre idea I had, and he looked at me and said, "I can't believe it! I've been feeling the exact same way!" With much prayer, many tears, and a lot of research, we made the decision to put Kathrynne in a small Christian school.

She was devastated when we broke the news to her. Actually, she was more than devastated—she was angry at us. Kathrynne was hurt and upset that we would choose to push her into a situation that was so scary to her. And my mama heart was torn up in pieces knowing how terrifying and upsetting it was for her.

As parents, it's our heart's desire to raise self-sufficient adults, not needy and dependent children. If we let our kids hide behind us, and we provide a thick barrier for them from anything that might be uncomfortable or difficult, we are actually doing our kids a massive disservice. They will never grow up and find the amazing fulfillment that comes from stepping out in faith and doing hard and scary things. They will also likely stay dependent upon us forever.

We knew if we kept letting Kathrynne stay where it was safe, she'd never grow a strong backbone or wings to fly. But knowing this and actually following through on a decision that terrifies your child—that's a whole lot harder!

I cried a lot that first day when we took her into school and then had to leave her there. That might sound weird considering she was going into sixth grade, but I knew how hard it would be for her. It took so much courage for her to even step foot in that classroom, let alone to actually stay there all day with a bunch of kids her age whom she didn't know.

The first few weeks were rough. She didn't like school. She dreaded going each day. And I spent a lot of time second-guessing our decision to throw her into the deep end instead of letting her stay in the shallow end with her life jacket on and Mom and Dad close by.

She and I had a lot of long conversations in those first few weeks. I told her often how much I loved her and how much I wanted the best for her. I communicated that I knew this took so much bravery from her, but that I truly believed she would someday look back and be grateful we made this decision.

She assured me that she would never look back and say it was the right decision. And I wondered, yet again, if she was right. But there was no turning back.

After those first few weeks, we noticed a small shift. She started talking more about people she was interacting with at school. She seemed a little bit happier and a lot less anxious about school drop-off each day. And we noticed that she actually seemed to be making a few friends.

Within a few months, those small shifts had turned into major changes. She built a few great friendships, was thriving at school, and began exuding a quiet confidence we had never seen in her before. Kathrynne no longer seemed awkward around kids her age and had started to believe that it was possible to have good friends.

We look at her now and can't believe she was once super shy and afraid of social interaction. In fact, she's the exact opposite now. She's a confident, outgoing teenager with more friends than we can keep track of and a social calendar we struggle to keep up with. Multiple times each day, I find her texting or talking with her friends, figuring out their next get-together. (The whole quarantining as a result of COVID-19 was a big challenge for her. She had to resort to spending hours video-chatting with her friends rather than getting to see them face-to-face throughout the week.)

I know not every child's story will have such a profoundly positive outcome like Kathrynne's, but I wanted to share three facets of letting go that have helped us on this journey with her—and with our other kids.

## Stop Parenting to Protect Your Reputation

As I've alluded to in previous chapters, for a very long time, having a good reputation with others was my primary parenting motivation. Of course, I didn't realize this was the root of much of my decision-making, but when it really came down to it, I was making most of my parenting choices through the lens of wondering, *What will other people think?*

It's hard to admit that, but it's true. I cared way more what people thought of *me* than I did about my kids' hearts.

As a result, I wasn't close with my kids. I didn't truly know their hearts.

Our relationship wasn't built on trust, and they didn't feel they could honestly share how they felt—because I would probably snap at them if I felt they weren't approaching something maturely enough.

There was very little grace in my parenting, and I carried around heavy guilt for how I was failing and for the ways my kids weren't living up to my expectations. I struggled to see the good because I was constantly frustrated by how they were falling short. I cared much more about what others thought of me than I did about how much my kids felt loved, cared for, and secure.

Every day, this approach was driving a bigger wedge between my kids and me. Since God revealed this to me, I've been working to always examine the motives behind my responses.

For instance, if I'm feeling frustrated with a child, I ask myself, "Where is this coming from?" Many times, it's because I've noticed some behavior in their life that is bothersome and instead of praying about it or having a gentle conversation with them, I'm playing out the worst-case scenario and what other people will think.

Or I'll often catch myself feeling the need to explain my kids' choices and decisions to others or to make sure people know that I'm working on a certain issue or character flaw with them. Why? In all honesty, it's pretty much always because I want to make sure others think I'm a good parent or think well of my child.

It's very common that I'll also catch myself getting ready to make a decision for my child based solely on what other people will think instead of what is actually best for my child.

Here's the thing: You are never going to please everyone and you are never going to get this parenting gig "right" in the eyes of others. That's not what matters.

What matters is that you seek the Lord, seek His wisdom for your child, and seek to love your kids well—even if that means other people look down on you, criticize your parenting, or question your decisions. I'd rather have a strong relationship with my child at the expense of my reputation with others.

> *I'd rather have a strong relationship with my child at the expense of my reputation with others.*

When Kaitlynn was eleven, she came to me one Sunday morning and asked if we could both wear our matching "fancy" dresses and high heels to church.

Truthfully, I was planning to wear a super casual outfit to church that morning, as I was feeling pretty blah, and part of me wanted to come up with an excuse to say no to the extra work it would require to get gussied up.

Plus, people don't really dress up much at our church, and I knew my fancy heels and chiffon dress would make me stand out.

But then it hit me: My eleven-year-old daughter wanted to match with me. This is a *gift*. Who cares if I stand out? Who cares if people wonder if I got my dates wrong and thought it was Easter?

Yes, it meant taking a little extra time, but the smile on her face and the excitement when she saw me all dressed up was so worth it!

Then, as we were walking into church, she reached for my hand to hold it. And I could see how crazy proud and happy she was to be matching her mom.

These days are fleeting. These moments are priceless. And this little choice I made to "say yes to the dress" was 100 percent worth it.

## Stop Micromanaging Your Child's Present and Future

The point of parenting is to raise adults to be sent out into the world to make a difference. But sometimes, I'm not so fond of thinking of that whole sending-out part. I want to keep my babies close to me forever!

I remember the first time we dropped Kathrynne off to go to a four-day overnight camp. She was just beginning seventh grade, and that small school we'd enrolled her in for sixth grade had a tradition of kicking off the school year for those in seventh through twelfth grades by going to a camp that was about an hour and a half away.

At that point, we had never done sleepovers or overnight camp, so this was a big deal. I found myself constantly wondering about her. Was she sleeping okay? Was she enjoying herself or feeling lonely or homesick?

Thankfully, parents and families are invited to come to the camp for a special evening halfway through camp week. I was so excited to get to see Kathrynne and was worried it might be hard for her for us to come and hang out with her and then leave again.

Well, I didn't need to worry! When we showed up for the parents' night, it took a while to even find her because she was having such a great time with a gaggle of girls. We ate dinner with her and then went to chapel with her and, while she was happy to see us, I could tell she was happy to be at camp and having a great time with her friends.

Clearly, she was doing just fine, and I didn't need to worry. That first four-day camp experience was so good for me. It proved to me that I was working myself out of a job—and that Kathrynne could function well without me.

It also reminded me that ultimately, I'm not in control of my kids' lives and decisions. I can do my best to make sure they are loved and cared for and nurtured, but I need to release them and their lives to God. My kids are His first, not mine.

Dr. Laura Markham offers this profound insight in her book, *Peaceful Parents, Happy Kids*: "Helicoptering comes from fear. Nurturing comes from love."[1] When we micromanage and bubble wrap our kids, we prevent them from learning to grow up and become adults.

> *Ultimately, I'm not in control of my kids' lives and decisions. . . . I need to release them and their lives to God. My kids are His first, not mine.*

At first, our kids will need us to stand very close to them as they navigate newness and risk-taking. But the older they get and the more they practice adulting, the more confident they will likely become.

As I've gotten better at letting go, I've had more and more of a desire to give our kids lots of opportunities to practice being adults. We've done this by encouraging our kids to

- **Be fully responsible for their own homework and projects.** From the time our kids were old enough to read and write, we let them be in charge of their own homework and school projects. They are always welcome to ask us for help—and they often do—but we don't oversee or micromanage their homework load or school projects. (As I mentioned earlier, this means that they sometimes turn in late work and they suffer the consequences of doing so.)
- **Email their teachers when they have a question.** We help them at first with this, but by the time they are twelve or

so, we expect them to be fully capable of doing this on their own. This is not only teaching them personal responsibility, but also the lost art of how to write and format an email.

- **Have difficult conversations with adults and peers.** We will give them counsel and suggestions, but we rarely step in and talk to a teacher, leader, or peer ourselves. We want our kids to learn to stand up for themselves, graciously confront situations, and feel confident to have hard conversations.

- **Contribute to our household.** From an early age, we expect kids to "earn their keep." This means helping with chores, being capable of doing basic cooking, cleaning, and laundry, and being willing to pitch in when asked.

- **Plan their own social events.** This one might seem a bit controversial, but it's been such a great thing for our kids—and they love it! If our kids want to have a party or have friends over, they are in charge of planning it. For birthday parties, we give them a budget, and they are responsible for planning the details, the guest list, the food, the activities. We help out where needed, but they do the bulk of the work. It's the same for having friends over or planning a gathering with friends. Our kids have been able to do this from the time they were about eight to ten years old.

The more opportunities we give our kids to take ownership and personal responsibility, the better we are preparing them for life. Part of real life involves struggle and difficulty. The older they get, the more they will experience the hard things in life, such as

- unkind people
- broken trust
- being ignored or overlooked or not chosen
- feeling they don't measure up
- feeling left out
- suffering consequences from poor choices
- having to learn things the hard way
- regretting decisions they made
- wishing they could get a redo on responses.

Over and over again, I've wanted to scoop my not-so-little babies up and take them far, far away to a safe world. I've wished I could take away their pain, magically get them to make the right choices every time, and protect them from hurt.

I find myself wanting to fix their struggles, shield them from the rawness and realness of humanity, carry their burdens and heartaches, or control what they know or experience. But I'm learning to just listen, to love, to ask questions, show empathy, and say, "Me too" when appropriate.

Most important, I want to let them know that no matter what, I'm in their corner. And I will always be—even on their darkest days.

## Start Saying Yes as Often as You Can

One of our kids asked to do something recently that would require a pretty big long-term commitment. I immediately wanted to respond with, "No, you can't do that!"

If I'm being honest, *no* was my go-to response as a parent for a long time.

Saying no is safer because, if I don't let my children try new things, I don't have to worry about them getting hurt or failing. Saying no is more convenient because it means fewer sacrifices of my time and schedule. It means fewer messes and interruptions and uncomfortable interactions with people I don't know (introvert here).

True, saying no might be safer and more convenient in the short run, but you know what it can do in the long run? It can drive a wedge of resentment between me and my child. It can cause frustration and make my child feel I don't care about their needs, don't trust them, and/or just want to stifle them from doing things.

The long-term consequences of my knee-jerk no's just aren't worth it when you think of it from that perspective.

There are times when we need to say no as a parent. But I want to be very careful and prayerful about those. I want to have a good reason for saying no and be able to clearly communicate it in a heart-to-heart conversation with my kids.

So, instead of instantly saying no recently, I said, "Let's talk about this. Why do you want to do this?" I asked a lot of questions and tried to really listen to their heart. We talked about the pros and cons of what saying yes to this would mean. We discussed the potential struggles this commitment could produce. We talked about the sacrifices they'd have to make.

And after a really great discussion, I said, "Yes, you can do this." And they were *so* excited and have been talking about it with such anticipation ever since then.

I don't know where this yes will lead. I know it's going to mean a pretty big commitment for this child and require a lot of schedule flexibility from me. But I know that it has communicated to my child, "I care about you. I'm listening to you. I trust you to make good decisions. And you're worth making sacrifices for."

I was inspired to say yes in this instance because of parenting advice I got from a wise older woman last year. She said, "Say yes as often as you possibly can. Unless it's truly a sin or a moral issue, try to always say yes."

She went on to say that if you rarely say no to your kids, they are much more likely to respect those no's when you say them—because they know it's an uncommon occurrence.

I try to remember this when my kids ask if they can have friends over last-minute or if I can take them somewhere or if they can attend some event or buy supplies for a new project. It's not usually easy or convenient, but I want to give my kids many opportunities to try new things, build relationships, exercise hospitality, and experience the world. And this means I need to be willing to make some sacrifices in order to say yes.

When we do say no, we try to always clearly communicate why we are saying no. I never want my reason to be "Because I said so." I want them to understand why I have a concern about a situation or why logistically it's just not possible to say yes. In cases when we do say no, I try to offer an alternative.

For instance, we are careful about allowing our kids to go to other kids' houses if we don't know the parents and family situation well. However, we are always happy to host kids at our house. So if one of the kids is asking about going over to the house of someone we don't know well, we'll encourage them to invite that child over instead.

(Note: I do think it's important to let you know that I draw the line on some things. For example, Kaitlynn would like to get a snake. I know that having a snake is not a moral thing—though

> *I want to say yes as often as possible. I don't want to spend this one shot I get at parenting shooting down my kids' ideas.*

could I make it one since the snake deceived Eve in the garden of Eden? I put my foot down about that one. Snakes in my house are a hard-and-fast no. Sorry, not sorry! But I happily said yes to getting her a pet hedgehog!)

I can't always say yes to every idea my kids have, but I want to say yes as often as possible. I don't want to spend this one shot I get at parenting shooting down my kids' ideas.

---

So, what happened to Kathrynne while she was in Suriname? Well, after eight days in that country and getting to experience some amazing and adventurous things (like hiking through the Amazon, teaching preschoolers at a local school, riding water buffalo, and staying in a house on stilts over the water!), her group was preparing to begin the long travel day home.

And that's when everything got turned on its head.

Suriname, up until this point, had no known cases of the coronavirus. But then, the day before Kathrynne's group planned to fly home, Suriname had their first case of COVID-19. In an attempt to slow the spread, the afternoon before the girls were supposed to fly home, Suriname shut its borders.

As in, no one could leave the country or get into the country. At all. For thirty days!

Here we had struggled to let our daughter leave for the nine-day trip, and now we find out she's potentially stuck there for at least thirty more days!

Despite this unexpected and unsettling news, I can honestly

tell you that my heart was at peace. Yes, I sincerely hoped that she wouldn't be stranded there for thirty more days and I missed her a lot, but I also felt peace knowing that she would be okay.

I knew she wasn't in any danger; she was with people who would take great care of her, and she has had international travel experience in the past. And I knew that she would look to the Lord and that God could take care of her much better than I ever could.

Sure, we still prayed fervently for doors to open for her group to get out of the country. Of course, we explored all the options of how to help her get home. And we absolutely were so grateful for modern technology and video-chatting so we could check in on her.

But I had deep peace in my heart that God was watching out for her. And He did. Thanks to the tireless work of some of the school administration and parents, plus government officials both in the United States and in Suriname, Kathrynne's group ended up getting on a special flight out of Suriname just two days later.

And guess what? She handled the whole thing like a champ. In fact, she told me she decided to focus on the positive in it instead of dwelling on the what-ifs and unknowns.

She came back stronger, more resilient, more independent (in a good way), more aware of the goodness and provision of God, and so incredibly humbled by how many hundreds of people were praying for her and their team to make it home safely. This experience is something she'll carry with her for the rest of her life—and it will likely serve as a reminder when she's in difficult and overwhelming or potentially scary situations in the future.

Letting go isn't easy, but it's one of the greatest and most loving gifts we can give our kids—especially when it comes to preparing them for their futures and adulthood. In addition, it's a tangible way we show our reliance upon the Lord and that we're parenting from a place of resting and trusting in the Lord instead of trying to control our kid's life.

There's so much more peace in that—as we'll talk about in the next chapter!

(Note: I have a helpful letting-go practice for you in the appendix. It's called the One-Minute Pause, and you can find it on page 211.)

## TWO TRANSFORMING TRUTHS
### for Love-Centered Parenting

1. Ultimately, I'm not in control of my kids' lives and decisions. I can do my best to make sure they are loved and cared for and nurtured, but I need to release them and their lives to God. My kids are His first, not mine.

2. I am never going to please everyone and I am never going to get this parenting gig "right" in the eyes of others. That's not what matters. What matters is that I seek the Lord, seek His wisdom for my child, and seek to love my kids well—even if that means other people look down on me, criticize my parenting, or question my decisions.

# Parenting from a Place of Freedom and Rest

I don't know what is wrong with me! I think I'm maybe going through early menopause or something!"

The words tumbled out of my mouth in a frustrated manner to my husband.

For the past few weeks, I had experienced a lot of weird symptoms—fatigue, headaches, nausea, an inability to focus, and extreme irritability.

I couldn't figure out what was going on.

It was August 2019. God had done so much work in my heart and in our family's life. Jesse and I had completely changed the way we approached parenting. Our family was so much happier. Our relationships with our kids were thriving. And our child who had been struggling so much had slowly become a completely changed individual—thanks to our parenting changes, therapy, medication, and the grace of God.

Don't get me wrong, we still had plenty of hard moments. I still reverted back to stressed-out parenting at times. I still needed to ask forgiveness of my kids on the regular. And we had our fair share of the normal teen and tween issues that every family faces.

But there was so much joy in our everyday lives. Laughter. Memories. And just plain enjoying our kids at a deep level.

Because of how God had changed my heart as a mom and because of the peace and joy we felt in our hearts and home, God had opened our hearts to pursue foster care.

We had spent the last four months taking classes, filling out stacks of paperwork, going through our home study, and prepping our home to become licensed as foster parents. After hours and hours of work and effort, it was our final walk-through week—and I was a hot mess!

As I shared in earlier chapters, God had transformed my heart from that of a legalistic and stressed mom to the heart of a love-centered mom. As a result, I had become a much calmer mom and I was usually able to juggle a lot without feeling stressed or overwhelmed. So this anxiety was strange—especially because everything was in order for the foster-care licensing walk-through. And it was just one simple, final visit.

Yet here I was, completely overwhelmed, irritable, and feeling totally frazzled about each tiny little thing. Jesse was taking the brunt of all my frustration—and he didn't deserve any of it.

I racked my brain to try to figure out what could be going on. Was I not getting enough sleep? Was I not taking care of myself? Was there something underlying that I was stressed about?

Nothing surfaced in response to these questions. Yes, I had a lot on my plate, but it wasn't any more than usual. Overall, I had been doing a great job of making space in my life for breathing room and rest.

What could it be? I realized my period was two weeks late, and then it hit me: Maybe all this craziness was early menopause.

I was only thirty-seven, but I'd heard of women starting menopause early. Jesse and I talked about it and he agreed that it was worth a call to my ob-gyn to see if they could get me in for testing to see if something was hormonally off.

But then we both looked at each other and he matter-of-factly said, "You know the first question they'll ask you when they find out that you're two weeks late for your period. They'll ask you if you've taken a pregnancy test."

Oh yeah, a pregnancy test. Jesse was right; that's the first thing they would ask.

"Ugh, okay. Well, why don't you go pick up a pregnancy test today and I'll take it so we can tell them that's not what it is?" I replied blandly.

Right about now, some of you might be confused. Why would I not have thought of taking a pregnancy test first? Why would I be so confident that I could not be pregnant?

## When God's Plans Look Very Different Than You Expect

Well, after Silas was born in 2009, we had hoped and planned to have more kids. But despite that desire and never using any form of birth control, I hadn't gotten pregnant.

For the first few years after his birth, my life was so full with raising three young kids and running a full-time business that I didn't think a whole lot about it. But as time marched on, and there was no positive pregnancy test, I started to wonder if we were ever going to have another baby. We had always assumed we'd have a large family. It seemed so weird that we'd have three kids in less than five years—and then nothing!

Five years went by, then six, then seven, then eight, then nine. I took countless pregnancy tests over those years. Multiple times we got our hopes up that this was the month . . . only to be disappointed again.

As our kids got older, they began asking for a little brother or sister. I didn't know how to tell them that I wanted so much to be able to give that to them, but it seemed like that dream was fading.

All around me, it seemed people were getting pregnant easily. Everyone just assumed we were happy with having three kids. Most people had no idea we were struggling with infertility. I kept pretty quiet about it because I wanted to be grateful for the three kids we already had, knowing so many were never even able to conceive.

However, our hearts still longed for another baby. So after more than nine years of trying and realizing our biological clocks were ticking, we decided it was high time we went to a fertility specialist.

I remember sending that initial contact form through their website to set up our first consultation. Their website made it sound like we would have to wait a few months to get in to see them, so I prepared myself to wait at least a few weeks to hear back.

To my surprise, they called me back in less than a day and offered us an appointment that week. They told me that most people wait months to get in, so this was pretty unheard of. All I could think was, *This is totally meant to be!*

We walked into the fertility clinic with so much hope and excitement. We were so sure that this was going to be our ticket to having another baby. And not only that, but we were hoping for at least two more babies.

We had the meetings, filled out all the paperwork, and scheduled all the initial tests. Some of the tests just involved shots and bloodwork; others were much more invasive. But we didn't care; we were committed to this.

After all of that was completed, the next step was to meet with the fertility doctor to get our Plan of Action. This was where they would map out the recommended next steps we should take—medicine, shots, intrauterine insemination (IUI), or in vitro fertilization (IVF). We were a little apprehensive, but also so excited. This was really happening!

We sat down in the chairs in the doctor's office, eager to hear what our Plan of Action would be. We had done a lot of research, and we were ready and willing to do whatever it took.

To our surprise, there was no Plan of Action suggested. Instead, there were only the devastating words that we weren't candidates for any of the treatments—not even IVF.

I'll never forget the gut-wrenching words from the doctor after he showed us in detail all of our combined issues. "You are welcome to try IVF, but you will just be wasting your money. There's no way we can create a healthy embryo from the two of you with the results these tests are showing."

They offered us the option of pursuing embryo adoption or getting a donor. I knew that—for a variety of reasons—neither was an option Jesse and I felt a peace about.

So with that, our dreams and hopes were dashed.

I walked out of that building so numb. When we got into the car, I started bawling. I sobbed deep, guttural cries the entire way home.

The kids were so excited to meet us at the door to hear about the new Plan of Action and when we'd be getting this baby thing on the road. I couldn't even look at them. I went straight to my bedroom, lay down on the bed, curled up in the fetal position, and cried until there were no more tears.

"Why, God? This hurts so badly! I was so sure you were leading us in this direction. Why is this door being slammed in our face?"

For a few days, I couldn't bear the thought of even seeing a baby or a young child. My heart was broken in pieces.

It took me a number of months to fully heal from the devastation. But over time, I was able to choose contentment. I chose to see that I had three beautiful gifts from God—and many, many people aren't able to conceive at all. I chose to trust that God was in this and there was something bigger and more beautiful here than I could see or understand.

After about six months, Jesse and I felt we were slowly getting to a place of closure and peace. As painful as the news was, it was also helpful to know that conceiving another baby was never going to happen. So we stopped hoping that every month would be the month, and we decided to embrace what our future was going to look like with three kids. We committed to throwing our lives into loving them well, parenting them even more intentionally, and being grateful for their lives.

Through a series of God-ordained events, over the next year our hearts were opened to the great need for foster parents in our area. We decided to sign up for the initial class to learn more. We never intended to become full-fledged foster parents, but we hoped to be able to find ways we could come alongside other foster families and serve them through respite care (watching the children they were fostering for short-term stints, usually for a weekend).

Once we attended the first few foster-parenting classes, we knew we couldn't just do respite care. We felt God strongly calling us to be licensed as foster parents.

We spent the next few months attending trainings, brushing up on our CPR, learning everything we could about fostering, baby-proofing our home, preparing our hearts emotionally and spiritually for what this might mean, having long conversations with our kids about this, going through multiple interviews and screenings, answering the same questions over and over again on different forms and in different meetings, installing locks on closets and cupboards, making space in one of our bedrooms to host children, and asking God to open our hearts to love well any and all children God would bring into our home.

It was scary to think of what stepping into this might mean—especially because I felt like the training sessions and home study process attempted to prepare you for worst-case scenarios. At the same time, we knew the dire need and could no longer turn a blind eye to it.

## A Completely Unexpected Surprise

After months of training and paperwork and inspections, our final home study walk-through week came—and here I was, an emotional, irritated wreck and wondering if I was experiencing early menopause.

Which is how I ended up in the bathroom on that Thursday morning, taking a pregnancy test so I could tell the ob-gyn, "No, I'm not pregnant."

Only, within thirty seconds of taking the test, a big, bold word popped up on the screen of the digital test: PREGNANT.

Say what?!

I sat there and stared at the test, sure I must be reading it incorrectly. Then I realized that I had never taken a digital pregnancy test before . . . maybe it says "pregnant" first and then it takes another minute or two for the word *not* to pop up on the screen and complete the phrase "not pregnant"?

So, I waited a minute. And then another minute. After the three full minutes the directions said it could take, there was still one big word on the screen: *PREGNANT*.

I was in disbelief. I called Jesse into the bathroom. "I think you might want to look at this."

The thought had never once crossed his mind that pregnancy was a possibility, so he was completely caught off guard.

We stood there laughing and crying at the same time. What in the world?! How had this happened?

I ended up taking a different kind of pregnancy test, just to be sure. Again, it was almost instantly positive.

*Little did I dream that God was going to give me the opportunity to parent a baby from birth again—and this time with a love-centered mindset!*

It took going to the doctor and seeing our baby's heartbeat the following week before I would fully believe it. And it took months and months for me to completely let it sink in: We were having a BABY!

The funny thing is, right before I found out I was pregnant, I had committed to write this book. Little did I dream that God was going to give me the opportunity to parent a baby from birth again—and this time with a love-centered mindset!

I wrote this on my Instagram account (@themoneysavingmom) and Facebook a few months into pregnancy:

"Will you parent your new baby any differently?" This is a question that a few brave souls have asked in the last 6 weeks since we announced our surprise pregnancy.

It's been 11 years since we've had a baby at our house and both Jesse and I have changed a lot in those 11 years.

We started our journey as parents so determined to do everything right. We worked so hard to make sure we were making good decisions and parenting well. We tried our very best. And I so often felt like a huge failure because I always came up short.

I carried around so much guilt and worked so tirelessly to put on a good front and look like I had it together. It was exhausting.

My greatest hope as I prepare to mother a newborn and toddler and grade schooler again (and as I prepare to be a foster mom, too—which will likely be happening soon!) is that I will focus a lot less on being right and a whole lot more on loving well, being present, and savoring each moment. And that I will parent to point all of my kids to Jesus instead of parenting for my reputation.

My kids don't need a perfect mom; they need a mom who loves well, shows up, and is willing to admit her struggles and shortcomings and need for Jesus.

I don't know what the next 11 years will hold, but I look forward with great anticipation to how I'm going to grow and change and become even a lot less worried about the things that don't matter and a lot more focused on the things that really do matter.[1]

- - - - - - - -

As I write this final chapter, I'm actually nine months pregnant with baby number four. And not only that, but I've also been writing it in the wee hours of the morning as I've been up with another tiny newborn—a sweet baby boy who was born prematurely who we are currently fostering. (More on that story in the epilogue!)

Two years ago, I was processing the loss of my dream of ever having another baby. Today, I sit here holding a sweet little sleeping newborn who is nestled up to my ninth-months-pregnant belly.

Only God, right?

"He himself bore our sins in his body on the tree, that we might die to sin and live to righteousness. By his wounds you have been healed" (1 Peter 2:24).

I think of all the healing God has done in my heart in the last few years. I think of how He has opened up my eyes to how much I am loved by Him. I think of His death on the cross and the redemption that I have in Him. I feel this sweet baby girl kicking inside of me. And my heart feels like it might burst with gratitude for the goodness and grace of God.

I've been thinking a lot about the gift of getting to parent from the beginning again and how I'll parent differently this time around. I wanted to close this chapter by sharing three lessons I've learned in recent years that will shape the way I parent—hopefully as a much gentler, calmer, love-centered mom.

## Embrace How God Has Wired You

In the early years of my parenting, I questioned my decisions a lot. I wanted to do everything "right" as a parent. I read books, I talked to other moms, I researched stuff on the internet, and I tried a host of other things.

Most of the time, I felt I was coming up so short. I just couldn't seem to figure out how to be organized, calm, happy, disciplined, motivated, put a great dinner on the table every night, stick with a tiny budget, dress my kids in cute clothes, look put together, stay healthy, have a great marriage, be involved in our community, invest in friendships, spend one-on-one time with each of the kids, have a well-decorated home, and stay on top of the laundry, cooking, cleaning, homeschooling, plus work full-time from home.

I'm sure it doesn't require a physics degree to figure out my problem. I was trying to be the Superwoman-est Superwoman who ever existed. And I kept beating myself up and feeling frustrated over falling short.

I would look around and see these other women who seemed like they had somehow truly discovered the secret to having it all together. What was my problem? Why did I always feel behind? Why were we always running late? Why was my laundry pile always so massive? Why did I constantly feel exhausted?

One day during this period, I had a little extra time and was perusing blogs. I stumbled upon this beautiful blog written by a seemingly amazing woman.

As I read her posts, I began to feel inadequate. She was pretty, fit, creative, and witty. She had a gorgeous home, had more children than I did, and seemed to have it all together.

I started to feel ugly, disorganized, out of shape, and like a pathetic woman by comparison. But I kept on reading—and felt even worse.

Then I landed upon a blog post where she talked about a woman she admired and wanted to be like. I was shocked when I clicked on the link and discovered the woman she was referring to was me.

Yes, this woman whom I felt I paled in comparison to wanted to be like me.

And then I realized how silly this was. Here she wanted to be me, and I was secretly wishing I were her.

It hit me anew just how easy it is to want what we don't have—a better house, a bigger yard, a stronger marriage, wiggle room in the budget, more creativity, or a different personality. There's always someone we'd like to trade places with because they seem to have what we want.

But trading places with someone wouldn't fix anything; we'd just inherit a new set of things we wish we could change. No one has it all together. Everyone has struggles and difficulties.

*Comparison only leads to discontentment.*

Comparison only leads to discontentment. We can't change who we are, but we can make the most of our situation. We can't choose the personality we are born with, but we can choose to embrace the personality we've been given and be intentional in using the gifts we have.

When we were going through our home study for foster care, one of the questions each member of our family was asked was, "Can you describe your family's core values?"

We each shared words and phrases that came to mind: "Faith. Family. Experiences over things. Standing up for the underdog. . . ." Everyone had a different angle on what our core values were, and I loved hearing the responses from Jesse and the kids.

However, there was one phrase we all said unanimously: "Never boring."

I went on to explain, "If you're looking for a family who is super organized and follows a really strict schedule, that's not us. But if you're looking for a family who thrives on adventure and rolling with the punches, you've come to the right house."

Some days, I wish we could be like the families who have the same bedtime routine and the same dinner time and the same wakeup time every day (and some of you are probably pretty surprised we have none of those things; all three vary at our house depending upon the week and the season of life we're in!).

But then I realize, I would probably feel bored and stifled by that—and so would Jesse. It's meant that we've jumped on a lot of last-minute and late-night adventures and that our kids are (usually) adaptable and willing to be along for the ride. My hope is that God will use our sometimes unconventional, rarely super-organized, and always up-for-adventure values to prepare our kids for what He has for them in their futures.

I definitely know that it has come in handy with all the un-known, unplanned, and unexpected situations that come along with foster care. It's also incredible to look back and realize how God has been preparing us for this for years.

By the way, if you're one of those much more organized people who has consistent mealtimes and bedtimes for your kids, that's also a fantastic gift you're giving to your kids. Honestly, I still often wish I could be you. But I'm learning I can be inspired by you and even challenged by you. It's also okay if our family chooses to have a more relaxed routine and approach to life.

How has God wired you? What are your family's unique traits and characteristics? What are your family's core values? I chal-lenge you to embrace these wholeheartedly and confidently hold to them—even if the way your family operates looks very different from how another family operates.

## Enjoy Your Kids

As I mentioned earlier in the book, our first three kids were born in less than five years. During that time, we also lived in three dif-ferent cities, my husband had five different jobs, and we started three different businesses. Needless to say, I spent a lot more time in survival mode than I did in savoring mode.

Looking back, I wish I had relaxed more, worked less, and just stopped to soak in the life right in front of me. Instead, I was always pushing myself—I "needed" to get the house cleaner, I "needed" to say yes to that really good business opportunity, I "needed" to do a better job of working out, I "needed" to get up earlier in order to get more things done.

I spent a lot of time stressed, working too many hours, and beating myself up over feeling like I was failing as a mom. (I hadn't yet learned how much I was loved by God and didn't understand what it looked like to live out of that love.)

I wish I had just stopped and savored the life right in front of me instead of constantly feeling frustrated that I needed to do better. However, since I can't go back and change those years, what I can do is live differently in the here and now.

I'm seeking to hold on to each day. Savoring the laughs. Cherishing the "I love yous" and times when my kids say, "Do you want to hang out with me, Mom?"

I'm also letting go of some of what I pictured things might be. I'm giving my kids space to make mistakes, develop close friendships, and not need me as they once did.

Some days are hard and frustrating. Some days are hilarious and amazing. Some days are sad and overwhelming. Some days feel holy and sacred and monumental.

Most days are a mixture of all of the above. And there's the constant tension between holding on and letting go. It's beautiful. It's challenging. It's good, this life right here in front of my eyes.

I don't want to miss it. I want to enjoy my kids—not only when they are babies learning to find their first smile, but also when they are teenagers and want to teach me a silly dance they learned on social media.

Multiple times recently, I've been told, "You just wait until your kids are teenagers. It's *so* much harder!"

Y'all, why is there this stigma surrounding teens? Why do kids over the age of twelve get such a bad rap?

I know that some of you are shaking your head thinking that I "only" have two teenagers and they are "just" sixteen and thirteen at the time of this book's publication. I get it that I still have a lot of teenager-raising years ahead of me.

But I refuse to buy in to the belief that the teen years have to be an awful experience.

Stretching? Yes!

Learning to let go? Absolutely!

Learning to be okay with them paving their own path and making mistakes? Sure.

Letting go of parenting for my reputation and instead parenting for relationship? That's my heart and greatest hope!

But let's stop proclaiming negativity over our kids' futures! Instead, how about we put that energy into loving our kids right where they are, believing the best about them, enjoying life with them, speaking life into them, and savoring the beauty of this calling of raising and nurturing the next generation!

## Choose Rest, Not Stress

"It doesn't matter how you played. It matters that you did your best."

This is what I told Silas as we walked to the car after a baseball game. He was feeling discouraged that he had made multiple errors in the outfield, which allowed the other team to get a few runs and ultimately win.

"Did you do your best?" I asked him.

"Yes, I did," he replied confidently.

"Well, then, you have nothing to be ashamed of or frustrated about. And regardless of how you played out there, I am and will always be proud of you."

Parenting reminds me often of how much I am loved by my heavenly Father. On those days when I stumble at life and make some big mistakes, He isn't standing there angry and frustrated and upset that I failed. He isn't mad at me when I don't have a home-run day.

His love and favor are not based on my performance—or even any action of mine at all. "While we were still sinners, Christ died for us" (Romans 5:8).

He isn't calling us to try harder or do better. He's calling us to rest in His love. To live as loved.

We are loved. Period. Not because of who we are or what we've done, but because of who He is and what He's done.

It's our tendency as parents to spend a lot of time worrying about our kids. I've lain awake at night worrying: *Am I spending enough time with them? Are they eating healthfully enough? Did I ask her the right questions in our conversation? Does she feel loved enough? Should I have responded to him like that?*

These worries can turn into full-blown anxiety, and I can quickly spiral into a place of beating myself up and feeling so much shame and guilt as a mom.

"Come to me, all who labor and are heavy laden, and I will give you rest" (Matthew 11:28).

He's whispering to you, "You are free. When I died on that cross, it was for you. It was for your mistakes and your mess-ups. It was so you don't have to carry around the weight of guilt and shame and feelings of not doing enough. Rest in me. Let me be adequate where you feel inadequate. Trust me in the messy, broken spaces. Look to me when you don't know how to respond or what the next step is. Lean on me when you feel overwhelmed with this job I've given you to raise these humans. Let me carry your burdens. Stop stressing and worrying and striving and trying so hard. I came to give you life and hope and joy. Rest in me. You are free!"

We don't have to parent out of shame, guilt, or the desire to impress others. The Gospel has freed us from the burden of trying to be a perfect parent with perfect kids. Our freedom is found in resting in Christ and His amazing love for us—even when we fail, fall, and make mistakes.

> *We don't have to parent out of shame, guilt, or the desire to impress others. The Gospel has freed us from the burden of trying to be a perfect parent with perfect kids.*

As Jeannie Cunnion wisely states, "Parenting is not about God relying on us to be perfect examples for our kids to follow. Parenting is about us relying on God to captivate our child's heart despite our mistakes."[2]

I walked into the room and saw a sight that perfectly summed up parenting: Next to my beautiful Mother's Day card from Silas and flowers from Jesse was a pile of dirty, bloody sheets on the coffee table (a child had a bloody nose the night before and had stripped their bed but the sheets hadn't made it to the laundry room yet).

This is parenting. It's beautiful and messy all at the same time. Some days it's glorious. Some days it's gross.

Many days, it's a mix of the marvelous, the mundane, and the messy all wrapped up in one big pile.

There are heavenly moments. There are heartbreaking moments.

There are days when I want to quit. There are days when I feel like, "This is the BEST job ever!"

Parenting is one of the hardest things I've ever done. It's stretched me beyond what I ever dreamed I was capable of. It's transformed me—a former stoic, stable, unemotional person—into a feeling, emotional, raw woman who can cry at the drop of a hat if it involves my kids.

I never knew the depths of love that existed until I became a mother. I never knew how impatient I could be either!

It's caused me to need Jesus like never before, and it's given me a glimpse of just how much my heavenly Father loves me.

Parenting has humbled me, broken me, and remade me.

It's taken me eighteen-plus years of marriage, sixteen-plus years of parenting, and a whole load of mistakes, but I'm a different person now—one who prioritizes people and relationships over projects and reputation.

I look back on these last four years and cannot believe how much has changed in my life.

I've fallen in love with motherhood at a much deeper level than ever before. Not because my kids have become more perfect or because I somehow figured out how to be a more perfect mom.

Mostly, it's because, more and more, I've been parenting from a place of rest and love. This has looked like:

- Recognizing even more how much I am loved by my heavenly Father. (When I bask in His love and acceptance, I am filled up to love my kids much more wholeheartedly. You can't give what you haven't received!)
- Letting go of my grand and unrealistic ideas of who I thought my kids were supposed to be and loving them for exactly who they are.

- No longer worrying so much about what other people think of my kids or my parenting. Instead, just leaning in and loving my kids in the middle of their hard questions, struggles, and frustrations.
- Preaching a lot fewer mini sermons and spending a lot more time listening and hanging out.
- Being okay with the tension that is often there when my kids ask difficult questions that I don't have answers for. Letting them grapple with their faith and convictions and giving them space and permission to come to conclusions different from mine.
- Opening the door for honest feedback and critique when they don't feel loved or safe or heard, and asking forgiveness often.
- Laughing together until we cry at ridiculous inside family jokes.
- Crying with them as they process loss and pain and hurt.
- Looking into their eyes.
- Listening to their stories.
- Hugging them often.
- Saying, "I love you."
- Calling out to God for wisdom and guidance to love these children well, in spite of my inadequacies and shortcomings.
- Believing the truth that God is with me, His Spirit is in me, and I don't have to do this alone or in my own strength.

Thank You, Jesus.

It's only because of understanding His love for me that I've been able to love my kids and husband more deeply and wholeheartedly than ever before.

God is not asking you to be a perfect parent, check all the boxes, or make all the right choices. He's asking you to rest and rely and fully lean on Him, look to Him for wisdom, trust Him with your kids, and leave your guilt at the foot of the cross.

> *Love-centered parenting means you can rest in His enough-ness. There's no guilt there, only freedom—to love your kids well, do the next right thing, and leave the results in God's hands.*

Love-centered parenting means you don't have to carry around the weight of feeling like you're not doing enough, because He is enough.

Love-centered parenting means you can rest in His enough-ness. There's no guilt there, only freedom—to love your kids well, do the next right thing, and leave the results in God's hands.

I hope my story inspires you to believe you can become a love-centered parent. You, too, can have this same peace and rest. You, too, can live as loved, because you are wholeheartedly loved by your heavenly Father!

## TWO TRANSFORMING TRUTHS
### for Love-Centered Parenting

1. God's love for me is not based on my performance. I can fully and wholeheartedly rely on His finished work on the cross.
2. Jesus came to give life and hope and joy. In Him, I am free—and I can rest in that.

# Epilogue

We pulled into the parking garage of the hospital. We were headed to the NICU to meet a precious little baby boy who needed a foster family to take him in as a long-term placement.

As we made our way to the entrance, my heart skipped a beat. I saw the sign—Psychiatric Hospital—with an arrow. It was almost four years since that terrible day we had taken our child to this very hospital and whispered, "My child is suicidal."

Four years.

So much had changed since then.

I stood there and looked at the sign, reflecting on how my struggling child had become so much calmer, emotionally healthier, and happier—and so had I!

I no longer was living my life worried about how my kids were going to turn out.

I no longer went to bed anxious and stressed over all the ways I had failed during the day.

I had so much more confidence in my parenting—even when others didn't agree with it or understand.

I thought about our kids—all four of them, including the surprise babe in my ever-growing belly. I realized how my relationships with them were now completely different.

Ever since I had stopped nitpicking and sermon-preaching, they had become so much more willing to share their hearts with me, to open up, to communicate their struggles and shortcomings, to come to me when they wanted to share something they had big feelings about.

Instead of being scared of the teenage years and what they might hold, I could genuinely say that they have been some of the best years so far. My teens love hanging out with me, love inviting their friends over to our house, and we have the best times together.

And I could hardly wait to meet this sweet baby girl I was due to deliver in just seven short weeks. We had dreamed so much about her future and couldn't wait to see what her personality was going to be like, how she would be different from our other kids, and even what she was going to be like as a teenager. I was looking forward to all of it—especially now that I had discovered a different way to parent and had seen how love-centered parenting had changed our home.

I stood there outside the hospital thinking about how all of this wouldn't have happened had I not hit rock bottom as a mom. Had my child not been asked to leave school and denied reenrollment. Had I not experienced months of agonizing about and praying over how to best walk with this child. Had my heart not been broken in devastation over what I had thought would be.

What seemed like the biggest blow as a mom actually turned into the greatest blessing. It had changed me from the inside out.

And here I was, back at the hospital again. This time not to head to the emergency room with a child who was suicidal, but to enter the NICU to meet a precious little baby boy we were going to become foster parents to.

We walked into the hospital and met with the social worker who was in charge of this baby boy's case. He had been born prematurely and had a number of medical needs as a result. He had been in the NICU for several weeks, and the doctors were hoping he could go home in the next few weeks, if all went well.

That's where we came in. The state was looking for a foster family who was willing to take him in for at least a few months, possibly longer. He would need extra love and care.

The doctors and nurses weren't sure what his long-term needs were going to look like or whether he would need ongoing therapy or what types of delays he might have. His case workers were hoping to find a family willing to be available 24/7 to care for him and love on him.

We had spent the last two weeks praying about bringing him into our home. We knew it wouldn't be easy—especially with me being so big and pregnant and soon delivering our own baby. We didn't know what it would be like to have two newborns at the same time, one who was medically fragile.

We wrestled through so many fears of the unknown and what the future might look like; we talked about what this would mean for our family and how everyone would have to make a lot of sacrifices, and we discussed how hard it would be to develop a strong bond with a baby and then give him back to his mama once she was able to take him back.

We all shared our concerns and we prayed a lot for clear direction and wisdom. At every turn, we felt so strongly we were supposed to say yes to this little boy, yes to the unknown, yes to the very likely weight of grief that would come from getting attached and having to say good-bye. So we said yes—even though we had no idea what that would mean or where that might lead.

We walked a maze of hallways with the social worker on that Wednesday afternoon to get to the NICU. My heart was beating fast the whole time, just thinking about meeting this little boy and all the unknowns. We finally made it to the NICU, signed in, slathered up with hand sanitizer, and walked into a room with multiple incubators to see a tiny little boy swaddled in a hospital blanket and in deep sleep.

And we instantly fell in love.

That was months ago. Fostering this adorable little boy has included a roller coaster of emotions, countless doctor's appointments and online meetings, a multitude of home visits and phone calls, a lot of crying out to the Lord for wisdom, and many days when thoughts of the unknowns and the future felt overwhelming. But I look back and have zero regrets.

This precious boy has brought enormous joy into our home. The late nights, the early mornings, the lack of sleep, the calendar full of appointments and meetings and therapy sessions, the tears over thinking of how much we love him and how hard it will be to give him back . . . it has been 150 percent worth every bit of it.

It has been an honor to get to pour love on him—knowing that ultimately, the goal is for him to reunify with his birth mama. I've realized that foster parenting gives you the opportunity to practice love-centered parenting at a whole new level. You get to lean in and love, listen well, lead with humility, and then—in most cases—completely let go.

You might never reap the fruit or see results from all of that love, but that's not the point. Your role is to love hard and big and sacrificially. To treat a child as your own as long as they are in your home. To advocate for them. To pray for them. To attach hard. And to be willing to have your heart broken when they leave.

Four weeks after we brought this tiny boy home from the NICU, our miracle baby—Kierstyn Michaela Paine—was born. When they put her little wet body onto my chest as soon as she was born, I lay there feeling like it was all a dream. It didn't seem possible that my body had just birthed this precious baby girl.

And it took Jesse and me a few weeks to really and truly come to terms with the fact that she is ours. That it wasn't just a dream. That at thirty-eight and thirty-nine years old, after more than a decade of hoping for another baby, we have the privilege of doing this parenting thing all over again from the beginning.

I'm humbled, grateful, and still a little bit in shock. But I'm also so excited for the future. Excited to mother a child from the start again—this time as a love-centered parent.

# Appendix:
# Practical Tools
# for Love-Centered Parenting

The resources for love-centered parenting in this appendix are designed to provide hands-on help to you in your journey. I have compiled a list of some of my favorite books that have deeply impacted me, a few songs I've listened to on repeat, Flare Prayers you can use at a moment's notice, a feelings chart to print out and reference, Conversation-Starter questions, details on the One-Minute Pause, and meaningful verses for you to meditate on and memorize. These resources are also available to download or print at CrystalPaine.com/LCP.

# LIVE LOVED MANIFESTO

Today, I commit to live as loved. I choose to believe I am fully and wholeheartedly loved by God for exactly who I am. I don't have to be more, do more, or achieve more to be loved by Him.

When I am tempted to believe the lies that have held me back for so many years, I will replace those lies with the truth that I am fully loved by God.

Jesus loves me unconditionally and doesn't judge me based upon my kids' behaviors or choices. I will put my hope in Him, not in my child's choices. I choose to be okay with my children making mistakes and messing up because I know this is why Jesus came.

I will focus on pointing my kids to Jesus and will no longer spend my days trying to be my children's rescuer and Holy Spirit.

I choose to open my tightly clenched fists trying to control all of life, and hold out my hands to accept the gift of God's love for me.

I refuse to believe the lies that tell me I'm not measuring up and am missing the mark of perfection as a parent. Instead, I choose to rest in the truth that I am created in the image of God and He sees me as His masterpiece. I don't have to beat myself up when I feel like I don't have what it takes but will remember that I am enough in Christ.

I was made for more than living a life stifled by lies and suffocated by false beliefs. I will replace those lies with the truth of who I am in Christ.

I am loved. I am forgiven. I am enough in Christ.

Jesus, thank You for loving me exactly as I am. Thank You for not expecting me to parent perfectly, but for being the Ultimate Example of a Love-Centered Parent to me.

I rest in Your amazing love for me. Let me be a conduit of God's love to others. May it pour through me and spill out to everyone I come into contact with.

# FLARE PRAYERS

Love through me, love of God.

Help me, Jesus, I can't do this by myself! But through You and Your strength, I can do all things.

God, make me a conduit of Your kindness to my kids today.

Spirit, give me wisdom right now. I need You. This is too big for me to carry on my own.

Jesus: Pour out Your grace and strength on me.

Thank You for Your love for me, Jesus. Let me rest in that love.

Heavenly Father, give me wisdom to love my child well right now. Let me walk with them and point them to You.

# FEELINGS CHART

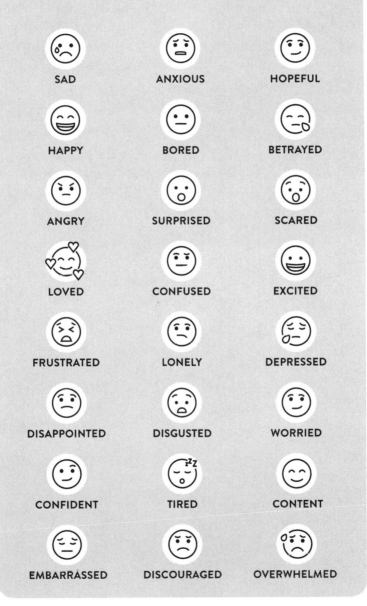

SAD

ANXIOUS

HOPEFUL

HAPPY

BORED

BETRAYED

ANGRY

SURPRISED

SCARED

LOVED

CONFUSED

EXCITED

FRUSTRATED

LONELY

DEPRESSED

DISAPPOINTED

DISGUSTED

WORRIED

CONFIDENT

TIRED

CONTENT

EMBARRASSED

DISCOURAGED

OVERWHELMED

# CONVERSATION STARTERS

What was the best thing that happened today?

What's making you happy right now?

What's a funny thing that happened today at school?

What made you smile today?

What was a time when I said something that confused/embarrassed/hurt you?

What do you think about _____?

What's your favorite thing we did this week?

What is something I do in my life that you are excited to do as an adult?

What would you change in the world if given the chance?

What do you think you will be doing ten years from now?

What are you feeling right now?

What do I do that makes you feel special?

Who was kind to you today?

What is your favorite memory?

Is there a time recently that you've felt misunderstood or hurt?

Tell me more about _____.

I'm curious to hear your thoughts about _____ .

How can I pray for you?

What was unexpected today?

What made you sad today?

What are you thinking about?

What do you want to be when you grow up?

What was one thing that made you laugh today?

What do you like most about _____ ?

On a scale of 1 to 10, how would you rate _____ ?

What is something you're thankful for?

Would you rather _____ or _____ ? (Can be silly or honest.)

# PLEDGE TO MY MATURING CHILD

## I PROMISE TO:

1. Stand on the sidelines cheering for you rather than trying to jump in and referee the game.
2. Provide a safe landing place for you as you practice flapping your wings, even though you will sometimes take a nosedive.
3. Watch you bravely step into new situations and sometimes make mistakes rather than paving the way for you to be 100 percent successful.
4. Remind you of the truth of who you are in Christ as you work on learning to use your voice and have hard conversations.
5. Ask questions to help you process rather than telling you the answers or what you should think.
6. Encourage you to grapple with your faith and convictions, not shy away from difficult questions, and come to your own viewpoints.
7. Celebrate and praise you for progress and tiny wins instead of constantly reminding you of where I feel you are falling short.
8. Listen much more and preach fewer mini sermons.
9. Embrace you for who you are instead of trying to fit you into a box or mold of who I thought you would be or think you should be.
10. Gently nudge you to step outside your comfort zone instead of allowing you to just play it safe and sit on the sidelines.

# THE ONE-MINUTE PAUSE

Feeling burdened, weary, tired, or heavyhearted today? Try the One-Minute Pause, an exercise I learned from John Eldredge (he shares more about this in his book *Get Your Life Back*). Here's how it works:

1. Set a timer for sixty seconds.
2. Take a few deep breaths.
3. Then verbally release the weight of what you are carrying. For example, say, "I release my stress or worry over my job to You, God." "I release my fear over my child's future to You, God." "I let it go."

Literally let yourself breathe out your fear, stress, worry, and tension and breathe in God's care and carrying of you.

This simple practice isn't going to solve all your problems, but it can certainly help you feel a little calmer and remind you that you don't have to carry the weight of the world on your shoulders.

God sees you. He cares about you. And He is big enough to carry your heaviest burdens. You are not alone.

# RESOURCES

## Recommended Reads

*A Gospel Primer for Christians: Learning to See God's Love* by Milton Vincent

*Good News for Weary Women: Escaping the Bondage of To-Do Lists, Steps, and Bad Advice* by Elyse Fitzpatrick

*Love Idol: Letting Go of Your Need for Approval and Seeing Yourself Through God's Eyes* by Jennifer Dukes Lee

*No Better Mom for the Job: Parenting with Confidence (Even When You Don't Feel Cut Out for It)* by Becky Keife

*Mom Set Free: Find Relief from the Pressure to Get It All Right* by Jeannie Cunnion

*Parenting: 14 Gospel Principles That Can Radically Change Your Life* by Paul David Tripp

*Parenting the Wholehearted Child: Captivating Your Child's Heart with God's Extravagant Grace* by Jeannie Cunnion

*Preach to Yourself: When Your Critic Comes Calling, Talk Back with Truth* by Hayley Morgan

*Families Where Grace Is in Place: Building a Home Free of Manipulation, Legalism, and Shame* by Jeff VanVonderen

*Raising Worry-Free Girls: Helping Your Daughter Feel Braver, Stronger, and Smarter in an Anxious World* by Sissy Goff

*Romancing Your Child's Heart* by Monte Swan

*Emotionally Healthy Spirituality: It's Impossible to Be Spiritually Mature While Remaining Emotionally Immature* by Peter Scazzero

*Sacred Rest: Recover Your Life, Renew Your Energy, Restore Your Sanity* by Dr. Saundra Dalton-Smith

*Say Goodbye to Survival Mode: 9 Simple Strategies to Stress Less, Sleep More, and Restore Your Passion for Life* by Crystal Paine

## Songs I've Played on Repeat

"What If" by the Ball Brothers

"Voice of Truth" by Casting Crowns

"Hello, My Name Is" by Matthew West

# MEMORY VERSES

*See what kind of love the Father has given to us, that we should be called children of God; and so we are.* (1 John 3:1)

*There is therefore now no condemnation for those who are in Christ Jesus.* (Romans 8:1)

*But you are a chosen race, a royal priesthood, a holy nation, a people for his own possession, that you may proclaim the excellencies of him who called you out of darkness into his marvelous light.* (1 Peter 2:9)

*For we are his workmanship, created in Christ Jesus for good works, which God prepared beforehand, that we should walk in them.* (Ephesians 2:10)

215

*Who shall separate us from the love of Christ?*
*Shall tribulation, or distress, or persecution, or famine, or*
*nakedness, or danger, or sword? As it is written, "For your*
*sake we are being killed all the day long; we are regarded as*
*sheep to be slaughtered." No, in all these things we are more*
*than conquerors through him who loved us. For I am sure that*
*neither death nor life, nor angels nor rulers, nor things present nor*
*things to come, nor powers, nor height nor depth, nor anything else*
*in all creation, will be able to separate us from the love of God in*
*Christ Jesus our Lord. (Romans 8:35–39)*

*So if the Son sets you free, you will be free indeed.*
*(John 8:36)*

*So you are no longer a slave, but a son, and if a son,*
*then an heir through God. (Galatians 4:7)*

*In this the love of God was made manifest among us,*
*that God sent his only Son into the world, so that we might live*
*through him. In this is love, not that we have loved God but that*
*he loved us and sent his Son to be the propitiation for our sins.*
*Beloved, if God so loved us, we also ought to love*
*one another. (1 John 4:9–11)*

*A soft answer turns away wrath,* but a harsh word stirs up anger. (Proverbs 15:1)

*In him we have redemption through his blood,* the forgiveness of our trespasses, according to the riches of his grace. (Ephesians 1:7)

*Have I not commanded you? Be strong and courageous.* Do not be frightened, and do not be dismayed, for the LORD your God is with you wherever you go. (Joshua 1:9)

*He himself bore our sins in his body on the tree,* that we might die to sin and live to righteousness. By his wounds you have been healed. (1 Peter 2:24)

# Notes

## Chapter 2: This One Truth Will Change Your Parenting

1. Hayley Morgan, *Preach to Yourself: When Your Inner Critic Comes Calling, Talk Back with Truth* (Grand Rapids, MI: Zondervan, 2018), 121–122.

2. Genesis 1:31.

3. Daniel J. Siegel, MD, and Tina Payne Bryson, PhD, *The Whole-Brain Child: 12 Revolutionary Strategies to Nurture Your Child's Developing Mind* (New York: Bantam, 2011), 99.

4. Siegel and Bryson, *The Whole-Brain Child*, 99.

5. Morgan, *Preach to Yourself*, 140.

6. John 19:30.

## Chapter 3: Live as Loved

1. *Trim Healthy Podcast* with Serene and Pearl, Episode 59—Face Plant!

2. Jeannie Cunnion, *Mom Set Free: Find Relief from the Pressure to Get It All Right* (New York: Howard Books, 2017), XXIV.

3. Amy Carmichael, *If: What Do I Know of Calvary Love?* (Washington, PA: CLC Publications, 2011), 35. First published 1938 by SPCK London.

4. Monte Swan with David Biebel, *Romancing Your Child's Heart* (Loyal Publishing, 2002), 239.

5. Becky Keife, *No Better Mom for the Job: Parenting with Confidence (Even When You Don't Feel Cut Out for It)* (Bloomington, MN: Bethany House, 2019), 54.

6. Brené Brown, *Rising Strong: How the Ability to Reset Transforms the Way We Live, Love, Parent, and Lead* (New York: Random House, 2017), 79.

## Chapter 4: Your Job as a Parent

1. Jeannie Cunnion, @jeanniecunnion, Instagram, February 19, 2019: https://www.instagram.com/p/BuE07Y5Bpuc/.

2. Crystal Paine, @themoneysavingmom, Instagram.com, September 28, 2017, https://www.instagram.com/p/BZmyxyzn3e-/v.

## Chapter 5: Lean In and Love

1. Laura Markham, *Peaceful Parent, Happy Kids: How to Stop Yelling and Start Connecting*, read by Xe Sands (Tantor Audio, 2013) Audible audio ed., chap. 1, 49:49.

## Chapter 6: Listen Well (aka How to Get Your Kids to Actually Talk to You)

1. Laura Markham, *Peaceful Parent, Happy Kids: How to Stop Yelling and Start Connecting*, read by Xe Sands (Tantor Audio, 2013) Audible audio ed., chap. 1, 25:01.

## Chapter 7: Lead with Humility

1. Cindy Rollins, *Mere Motherhood: Morning Times, Nursery Rhymes, and My Journey Toward Sanctification* (Concord, NC: CiRCE Institute, 2016), chap. 13, Kindle.

## Chapter 8: Let Go (aka Raising Adults, Not Kids)

1. Laura Markham, *Peaceful Parent, Happy Kids: How to Stop Yelling and Start Connecting*, read by Xe Sands (Tantor Audio, 2013) Audible audio ed., chap. 5, one-hour mark.

## Chapter 9: Parenting from a Place of Freedom and Rest

1. Crystal Paine, @MoneySavingMom, Facebook.com, October 22, 2019, https://www.facebook.com/MoneySavingMom/posts/10157045845788227.

2. Jeannie Cunnion, *Mom Set Free: Find Relief from the Pressure to Get It All Right* (New York: Howard Books, 2017), 15.

**Crystal Paine** is the founder of MoneySavingMom.com, host of *The Crystal Paine Show* podcast, *New York Times* bestselling author of *Say Goodbye to Survival Mode*, and author of *Money-Making Mom.*

Her desire is to help women across the globe live with more joy, purpose, and intention in their everyday lives. She lives with her husband and kids in the Nashville, Tennessee, area, where she is actively involved in her local church. Her biggest passions are helping women understand how the Gospel can radically transform their lives, raising awareness for foster care, going on adventures with her family (locally, domestically, and internationally), finding great deals at the grocery store, heartfelt conversations, and trying to read too many books at one time!